Cover: American Modern covered
pitcher (Chartreuse Curry), water
pitcher (Coral), and gravy boat
(Granite Grey), designed 1937.
Photographed by Courtney Frisse.

Russel Wright

AMERICAN DESIGNER

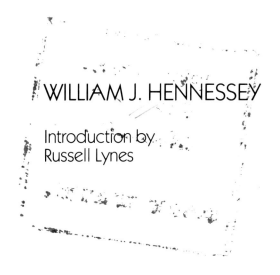

WILLIAM J. HENNESSEY

Introduction by
Russell Lynes

Gallery Association of New York State

The MIT Press
Cambridge, Massachusetts
London, England

This book accompanies an exhibition circulated by the Gallery Association of New York State. The project was made possible by a grant from the National Endowment for the Humanities. and by the New York State Council on the Arts and New York Council for the Humanities. The Walter Foundation provided additional funding for this book.

Design by Melanie Roher Design. Inc.
Photography by Courtney Frisse. Paulus Leeser.
and Steven Tucker
Typography by DM Graphics. Inc.
Printed by Monroe Litho Inc.. Rochester. New York

Printed and bound in the United States of America

Library of Congress catalog card number: 83-61215
ISBN 0-262-58066-7

Contents

Acknowledgments

My mother and father purchased their Russel Wright furniture and American Modern China when my father returned from the war in Europe. Years later, after I was graduated from art school, I realized that, in the absence of written history on industrial design, Russel Wright—the American institution I grew up with—had gone so far unnoticed. Few people my age recognized his name. Peter Langlykke, founder of the Gallery Association, and I used to fantasize about organizing an exhibition that would fill this gap. Then, five years ago, Paul Walter, collaborating with the Gallery Association on another venture, served me lunch on Russel Wright dishes. The exhibition seemed destined to come about.

Since then the project has taken shape more systematically with the help of a number of professional people. William Hennessey, then Director of the Vassar College Art Gallery, did the research into Wright's work, planned the exhibition, and wrote this book. Stephen Horne, then Gallery Association Registrar, and Helen Kebabian, Exhibitions Coordinator, applied to the National Endowment for the Humanities Museum Program for the grant that funded the exhibition.

Gallery Association staff, Helen Kebabian with Connie Klein, Exhibitions Assistant, and Bruce Moseley, Registrar, organized the exhibit and this publication; Mirko Gabler, Designer, designed the exhibit to fit various museum settings; Todd Dresser, Michael Lloyd, and Ben Critton, Art Preparators, fabricated the various components of its display. Sue Bauman, Fiscal Manager, and Cindy Jones, Assistant to the Director, provided fiscal and administrative skills; Donna Lamb, Art Transit Coordinator, with the Gallery Association's Driver/Art Handlers, Bill Burgess, Irv Durling, Dave McKean, Nicholas Purdy, and Dave Swetland transported the artifacts safely to each site. This brief account of their various contributions can hardly acknowledge the importance of the expertise and commitment they brought to the project.

Finally, Sara Blackburn provided invaluable assistance in the editing of the manuscript. Russell Lynes wrote the introduction. Distribution is being handled by the MIT Press through the particular efforts of Roger Conover.

Special thanks must also go to those friends, consultants, and collectors of Russel Wright whose hospitality and generous offering of information, time, artifacts, and memories have made this publication and the exhibition possible: Ann Wright, Arthur Pulos, Margaret Spader, Carol Franklin, Ray Spilman, Marley Beers, and Al Fromberger.

We are indebted also to the following institutions and curators for their willingness to extend the resources of their museums to other institutional settings: Carolyn Davis, Curator of Manuscripts, The George Arents Research Library for Special Collections at Syracuse University; Dianne Pilgrim, Curator of Decorative Arts, The Brooklyn Museum; David Revere McFadden, Curator of Decorative Arts, The Cooper-Hewitt Museum of Design; Marceline McKee, Coordinator for Loans, The Metropolitan Museum of Art; J. Stewart Johnson, Curator of Design, The Museum of Modern Art.

We appreciate the generous loan of artifacts from the following galleries and private collectors: Marley Beers; Joe Chapman; Michael Smith, Depression Modern; Chris Kennedy, American Decorative Arts; Rosalind and Irving Richards; Paul F. Walter; and Ann Wright.

In creating *Russel Wright: American Designer*, it has been the generosity of the National Endowment for the Humanities, the New York State Council for the Arts, and the New York Council for the Humanities that has ultimately made this project possible. Once again, The Walter Foundation stepped forward with a timely and generous gift toward this publication.

Kevan N. Moss
Executive Director
Gallery Association
of New York State

Russel Wright: American Designer would not have been possible without the generous cooperation and assistance of many individuals. I would particularly like to thank Ann Wright (Russel's daughter, involved in and supportive of the project from the start), Irving Richards and Herbert M. Honig (one-time business associates), and Margaret Spader, Joseph Chapman, and Carol Franklin (Russel's friends). Marley Beers shared her large Wright archive freely with me and Carolyn Davis was most helpful in making the Wright papers in the Syracuse University collection available to me. Arthur Pulos, Raymond Spilman and Russell Lynes were similarly forthcoming with their reminiscenses of Wright and his context.

At Manitoga, Susan Eirich-Dehne, Peter Keibel, and Philip Mayberry gave up many hours acquainting me with the mysteries of the park and house. Sara Blackburn carried out much-appreciated editorial work on the manuscript and Kevan Moss and Helen Kebabian of the Gallery Association could not have been more supportive. Finally, to my wife, Leslie, goes heartfelt thanks for patience, advice, and understanding.

William J. Hennessey
Lexington, Kentucky

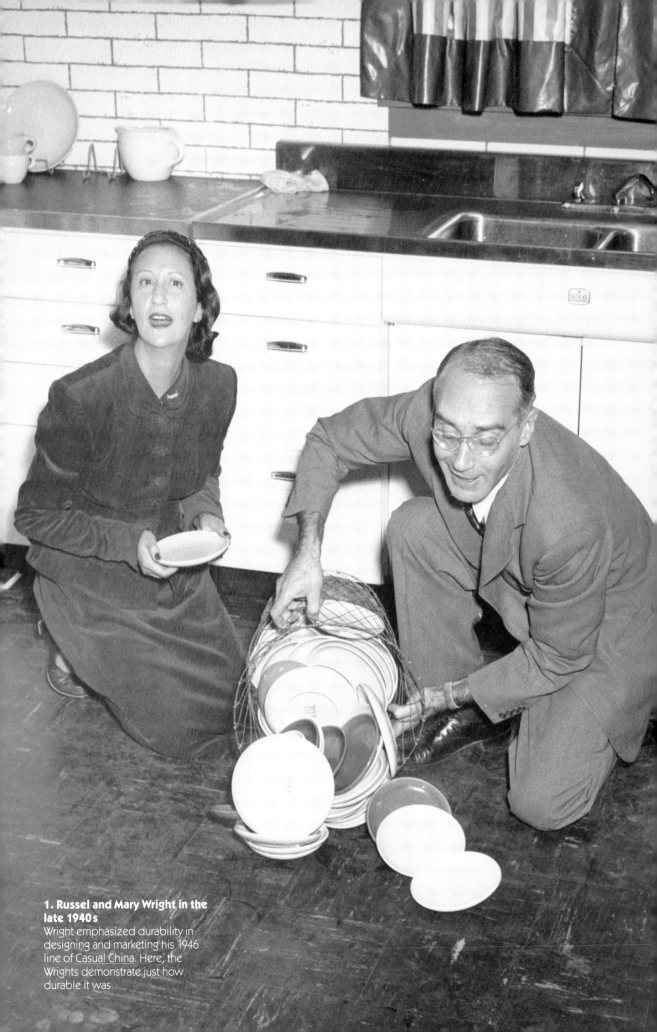

1. Russel and Mary Wright in the late 1940s
Wright emphasized durability in designing and marketing his 1946 line of <u>Casual China</u>. Here, the Wrights demonstrate just how durable it was.

Foreword

My first encounter with the designs of Russel Wright, most particularly with his furniture and tableware, was not quite half a century ago at Macy's department store in New York. This was in 1934, not the worst year of the Great Depression whose terrors were announced to an optimistic America by the crash on Wall Street on October 29, 1929, but it was bad enough. It was a time of 25¢ movies and 25% unemployment. It was the era of the Model "A" Ford, and the demise of the "tin Lizzie," as the Model "T" was affectionately called. It was also a time when Hollywood began to speak to us with sound synchronized with sight, and when movie stars whose virtues were their looks and those whose voices squeaked sank into obscurity, fallen heroes and heroines.

The 1930s, when Wright first hit his stride, was also the decade of the newly completed Chrysler Building with its shimmering top and a spike to pierce the New York sky, put there to confirm its claim as the tallest building in the world...which, briefly, it was. Its gargoyles were giant replicas of Chrysler radiator caps. It was also the decade of the Empire State Building, which exaggerated its height with a tower to which dirigibles (then thought to be the future of air transport) and blimps were to anchor, but never did because of updrafts that no one had thought to anticipate much less compute.

It was the era of Art-Deco, which got its name and much of its kudos from the Exposition Internationale des Arts Décoratifs et Industriels Modernes in Paris in 1925, a style that was attacked by those who regarded it as "dishonest" because it was "superficial" and had nothing to do with the newly revitalized "functional" design as promulgated by Walter Gropius of the Bauhaus and preached by the Museum of Modern Art, which opened for business just a month after the Wall Street crash. The Museum conducted an energetic campaign for "good design," and it had shocked the critics and much of the public first by its exhibition of "International Style" architecture in 1932 (Alfred Barr, the museum's director, had given the style its name) and then, two years later, by a "Machine Art" exhibition organized by Philip Johnson, not yet an architect. It made much of the beauty and elegance not just of the machine-made objects whose simplicity and clarity of design Johnson admired, but of parts of machines themselves—ball bearings, airplane propellors, steel springs. The show also included household equipment such as kitchen drain boards, lamps, and tableware: among them were pieces by Russel Wright.

It is difficult to capture in retrospect the energy of the dispute between those who delighted in Art-Deco—who greatly admired the Chrysler Building and Radio City Music Hall with its decorative furnishings by Donald Deskey—and those to whom it represented a betrayal of good functional design. "Modernistic" was the blackest epithet the Museum of Modern Art could heap on Art-Deco. It meant an applied style, a sort of fancy slipcover for the kind of honest design that grew from the properties of materials and the true function of the piece, whether it was a table or a skyscraper or a toaster. It was tarted-up "modern," using some of functionalism's formulas but making them more palatable to the public by applying geometric ornament with a somewhat mechanistic flavor that might have been borrowed from the famous German film, *The Cabinet of Dr. Caligari*, or

**2. Russel Wright and staff in the
1930s**
The young designer surrounded by
his staff in his first New York office.

inspired by George Antheil's *Ballet Méchanique*. It also borrowed wind-resisting forms from trains and planes. Radio sets were "streamlined," and so were Scotch-tape dispensers and steam irons to make them look racy and up to date. Bookcases were "stepped up" like the day's skyscrapers, which were subject to building codes that required that every so many vertical feet there be set-backs lest city streets become dark canyons into which only fine slices of daylight might fall. Blue glass mirrors were shaped like spiky fans. Standing lamps were something between plumbing and calla lilies.

One of the reasons why Art-Deco was so successful in America in the 1920s was that it reflected the instability and fun of fashion rather than the more subtle and austere qualities of style. Art-Deco (also called Art Moderne) had taken a little of this and a little of that, a little Wiener Werkstätte, a little Art Nouveau, a pinch of Bauhaus, a dash of Cubism and a few grains of Futurism and de Stijl and combined them with a kind of frivolity that suited the Frenchified taste of the 1920s. Wright, on the other hand (though there are occasional traces of Art-Deco in his work) was interested in making designs that followed Bauhaus principles. He concerned himself with producing American design that Americans could accept not because of any rigid doctrine of functionalism but because, to use a Quaker phrase, "it spoke to their condition."

Russel Wright was the answer for those of us who were brought up to accept the Bauhaus doctrine as announcing the design wave of the present and the hope of the future, but who could not afford to buy the expensive imports of Le Corbusier and Mies van der Röhe and Marcel Breuer. Wright's furniture, and his dishes and bowls, ice buckets, pitchers, and flatware spoke to us in straightforward language that we could enjoy and accept as honest. What was perhaps equally important, we could acquire them gradually and add them to the miscellany that we had bought second-hand or been given. They seemed to be at home with Victorian and especially with Mission pieces. Two of the pieces of Wright furniture we bought from Macy's in 1934, a double bed and a chest of drawers, are still serving their purposes. So are a number of pieces of his pottery—most particularly dinner and salad plates and shallow bowls. In forty-nine years cups and saucers have disappeared (I was never fond of the cups; the handles didn't accommodate themselves to human fingers, at least not to mine), but we have replaced plates when we could find them, sometimes in the pleasant gray they were when we first bought them, and the yellow-green ones.

We were not alone then in our pleasure in Wright's designs—or more specifically in the accommodating and handsome artifacts that he made it possible for us to buy—and we are not alone today. In the 1930s (our twenties) when we came on a bargain, we shared our discovery as our friends shared their discoveries with us. We were, as a consequence, members of the "Russel Wright crowd," and pleased with ourselves for our perception. Ours was, I assure you, no small clique. We were part of the mass market for which Wright designed and proud of it, perhaps partly, I confess, because we thought we had got there before the rush. Just the other day I mentioned this exhibition catalogue to the curator of Decorative Arts of a distinguished museum, a man half my age, and he was delighted to tell me that he had recently discovered in a shop in the middle west a "complete Wright dinner service" which he had snatched up for his own collection. Truly good designs do not date.

Wright was born in Ohio soon after the turn of the century. His family were Quakers, and this condition may have accounted in some degree for his attitude toward design. There was a consistent directness and lack of ornament, a strictness of a sort, about his work that it is not unreasonable to suppose was bred into the young man whose ambition was to be an artist. It was appropriate to his talent and temperament that he should shift from painting, which he first studied, to sculpture which, as a designer in three dimensions, he practiced throughout his life. He was early involved with the "little theatre" movement in New York through the encouragement of Aline Bernstein, the influential theatrical designer. She found him a gifted and attractive young man and introduced him to the make-believe world of the stage, which was not very distant from the make-believe of commercial display which he later practiced skillfully to promote his own designs.

Wright was both an honest and shrewd designer. He liked to work with natural materials, wood and clay and aluminum primarily, and extract from them a simple and subtle elegance in shapes that were as useful as they were discreet. His position as a designer was somewhere between the European socio-political stance of the Bauhaus and his devotion to the crafts movement as it evolved in the late years of the nineteenth century and the early years of this one. Wright was no social reformer in a political sense, but he was a crusader nonetheless. Through the medium of his work it was his mission to provide Americans with comfort, efficiency and esthetic pleasure at a reasonable price and to convert them to his concepts of the useful and beautiful for the enjoyment of their surroundings.

I had the pleasure of lunching in New York with Wright and an architect neighbor and friend of his and mine about a dozen years ago. I found him a rather reserved, perhaps shy, man not given to talking about himself or his work but eager to talk about educating young designers and consumers and about the conservation of natural resources. I wondered at the time if he thought of himself as something of a "period piece" who had lost his talent to surprise, and found that what he had crusaded for in design had been absorbed into convention and taken more or less for granted. If he did, it was the price of his success, of having accomplished what he set out to do.

It is not the purpose of this Foreword to do more than encourage you to read Mr. Hennessey's interesting and perceptive introduction to Russel Wright, his career in the theater and architecture and industrial design and his varied and often beautiful work. He enriched my generation (which was also his, give or take a few years), and he introduced us to new optical and physical pleasures that have stayed with us. But above all, in my judgment, he was exactly right for his time. In the early thirties we entered a period of informality that was very different from the starched Edwardian decades and the frenetic twenties. We put aside, partly for financial reasons but also for humane and social reasons, a good many conceits of behavior that were regarded as *de rigeur* by our parents' generation.

Our manners changed (I do not mean that they deteriorated, though our parents would have thought so, as parents inevitably do), and we changed our ways of entertaining our friends and ourselves and of enjoying our leisure. Russel Wright not only saw that this change was in the cards, but he abetted it. In so doing, he did us a favor that those of us who benefited from it will not forget.

Russell Lynes

P.S. As a two-"l" Russel, I asked Wright why he spelled Russel with only one "l" and he told me that he was baptized with two. When he ordered some letterheads years ago, they had come with just one. "That seemed to be distinctive," he said, "so I adopted it."

Russel Wright
AMERICAN DESIGNER

Forty years ago the words "designed by Russel Wright" on a set of dinnerware or a piece of furniture insured instant recognition. Wright was easily the best known designer in America; his name was a household word. By designing and successfully marketing inexpensive, mass-produced consumer goods, he played a key role in leading middle-class Americans towards an acceptance of modern design. The sophisticated marketing programs that promoted his work to popular success linked American design and manufacture with patriotism and with the lures of modernity and efficiency. By theatrically exploiting his name as a sales tool, Wright built an enormous and loyal following. Yet the significance of his work extends far beyond its extraordinary commercial success.

In addition to his major importance in the history of industrial design and in the evolution of popular taste in America, there can be no doubt of the originality and the intrinsic quality of Wright's ceramics and furniture. His inventive and highly personal designs are collected today by a comparative few; they deserve to be better known.

Wright was a man of complex character. He was so shy that he was almost reclusive, yet he did not hesitate to promote his designs through personal appearances. Fiercely independent and jealous of his privacy, he depended all his life on the guidance of his wife and friends. He also relished his fame, although it did little to allay his deep personal insecurity and sense of isolation. Indifferent to business affairs and sometimes almost hostile to them, he enjoyed considerable financial success. In many ways absent-minded and disorganized, he was capable of orchestrating every detail of a complex design commission. By the time he died in 1976, he had long outlived the celebrated status he had achieved.

Wright's career was also characterized by extremes. His early designs were intended for an elite market, while his later work was decidedly populist in tone. His *American Modern* dinnerware, introduced in 1939, became the most popular ever sold, but it was followed by a debacle, the devastating failure of the marketing program he designed to promote the home furnishings line he

OPPOSITE
3. Russel Wright publicizes a new design, ca. 1948
Though a shy man, Wright did not hesitate to promote his designs through personal appearances. This publicity photograph introduced one of his ceramic dinnerware lines.

called the *American Way*. At the peak of his fame, Wright abandoned his New York design practice to retreat to his country estate, Dragon Rock, near Garrison, New York. He would spend the last twenty-five years of his life there.

Behind these apparent contradictions, Wright was, above all, a craftsman, one who responded warmly to nature and to natural material. He believed deeply in the unique character of American life and worked to design products that would fulfill specifically American needs. He possessed an unusual ability to dramatize the presentation of his works, and applied it by designing complete "stage settings" for individual pieces or lines, a talent that was presaged by his early work in the theater. As we follow his career, we can observe his steady evolution from hard, mechanical forms towards soft and organic ones, a development that parallels Wright's steady retreat from his active urban design practice to an almost exclusive involvement with the creation of his country retreat. At Dragon Rock Wright designed and created a total environment, much of it with his own hands, in which every detail was calculated and the separate contributions of man and nature became almost indistinguishable.

Wright's impact on American life extended far beyond his individual designs. Through his concepts of "informal hospitality" and "easier living," he played a major role in transforming basic American attitudes about entertaining and family life. His furniture designs liberated middle-class consumers for the first time from the convention of pre-chosen "suits" of furniture, and encouraged them to assemble rooms that were at once expressive of their tastes and adaptable to their own particular needs. With his *American Modern* dinnerware, Wright transcended the prevailing public resistance to modern styles with a mass-produced line of ceramics which was simultaneously contemporary in appearance, functional in design, low in price, and aesthetically acceptable to a wide range of buyers. By presenting himself as a creative artist, Wright raised the public status of the industrial design profession to a level approaching that enjoyed by such "fine arts" as painting and sculpture. In doing so, he furthered his long-cherished desire to correct what he saw as "America's artistic inferiority complex." Later, through his work with the National Parks Service and particularly at Dragon Rock, Wright extended his influence beyond home furnishings to encompass all aspects of our visual environment. By selecting and exploiting links between the industrial and fine arts, between one's home and the natural environment of which it is a part, and between Oriental and Occidental traditions, Wright established his importance as a major figure not only in the history of industrial design but in this country's cultural history as well.

This exhibition documents Wright's career, charts his development as a designer, and examines some of the apparent contradictions in his life and work. But its major purpose is to retrieve Wright's reputation from the comparative oblivion in which it now reposes, and to display and celebrate the freshness, beauty, and whimsey of his best designs.

Early Life

Russel Wright was born on April 3, 1904 in Lebanon, Ohio. The family was an old and established one: his mother was related to two signers of the Declaration of Independence, and his father, a Quaker, was a local judge.[1] Wright's first important contact with the art world came in 1920, when he enrolled in Saturday and summer art classes at the Cincinnati Academy of Art. He was able to study briefly with the painter Frank Duveneck before Duveneck's death that same year.

Russel's father was insistent that his son enter Princeton (his alma mater) to prepare for the study of law, but because Russel was only sixteen when he graduated from high school in 1920, he was allowed a year in which to pursue his growing interest in art. Wright moved to New York City during the fall of 1920, eager to take advantage of his reprieve. He enrolled immediately at the Art Students' League and began to study painting with Kenneth Hays Miller. Wright's instructor was not impressed with his pupil, however, telling him that he seemed to "carve" the canvas.[2] Russel took the hint and transferred to a sculpture class, where his success was immediate: after only two weeks' study, he entered a student competition to design a war memorial and won first prize.

The summer of 1921 found him on Martha's Vineyard as tutor to the children of the painter and draftsman Boardman Robinson. When he entered Princeton the following fall, Wright immediately missed the excitement of New York City bohemian life, but found a ready substitute in the Princeton Triangle Club, where he was active as both a theatrical designer and director. He spent the summer of 1923 at the Maverick Art Colony in Woodstock, New York, designing for the Maverick Festival, which was held at Hervey White's farm and cottage colony every August on the night of the full moon.[3] The festival's theme that year was the circus, and Wright designed a set of large papier-mâché animals as props: they were to be "recycled" later in his career.

Back at Princeton in the fall, Wright continued his work with the Triangle Club, helping to mount productions of *Drake's Drum*, *Hamlet*, and *Romeo and Juliet*. He also contrived to spend nearly every weekend in New York City as an apprentice to the designer Normal Bel Geddes, who was preparing the celebrated production of *The Miracle*.[4] Bel Geddes himself was soon to abandon theatrical work for industrial design, and the experience of working with him was clearly an important one for the young Wright.

At Princeton, Wright's indifference to academics became more and more obvious. He left early in 1924, committed to a career in the theater. For financial reasons Wright could not accept Bel Geddes's offer to take him on as a full-time, but unpaid stage design apprentice. At about this time Wright met the theatrical designer Aline Bernstein (later the mistress of Thomas Wolfe) who became his close friend and mentor. He accompanied her on a brief but romantic trip to Europe in 1925. Wright credited Bernstein as a key influence on his early career. She taught him not only practical skills of scene and costume design, but shaped his aesthetic personality as well. With Bernstein's help, Wright secured a job at the Neighborhood Playhouse in New York. He later moved on to the Laboratory Theatre, an enterprise patterned on Stanislavsky's Moscow Art Theatre, and stage-managed a few Broadway plays before returning to the Maverick Theatre in Woodstock for the summer of 1927. By this time the Maverick Festival had become more organized and respectable, offering regular theatrical productions. It was in Woodstock that he met Mary Small Einstein, a sculpture student. Her wealthy and socially prominent family was not enthusiastic about their marriage, which took place the following fall in New York.

Wright's marriage was one of the turning points of his life. Almost at once Mary began urging him to adapt the experience and training he had received in designing and fabricating theatrical properties to producing decorative objects for retail sale. Wright spent most of 1927 stage-managing the Theatre Guild productions of *Marco Millions* and *Strange Interlude* before moving on to Rochester, New York as stage manager of George Cukor's theater company there. The Wrights' hectic and nomadic life with Cukor convinced Russel to take his wife's vocational advice. Upon returning to New York from Rochester, they consolidated their savings and moved into an apartment at 18 Beekman Place, still an inexpensive neighborhood at the time.[5]

Still naive, and with a total lack of business experience, Russel plunged into a new career. He began by working on life-sized caricature masks of celebrities, executed in a variety of materials: Greta Garbo in plastic with spun glass hair, John Barrymore in mirrored glass, or Herbert Hoover fabricated in marshmallows. Mary's attempts to sell these creations to Madison Avenue gift and specialty stores were unsuccessful, although several of the caricatures were published in the *New Review*.[6] Wright's miniature plaster animals, modeled on the ones he had originally designed for the Maverick Festival, proved to be more appealing. The painted and decorated beasts were initially sold to Rena Rosenthal for her Fifth Avenue specialty shop. As the animals became increasingly popular, Wright expanded into other materials, including aluminum and chromium-plated sheet metal. Cut from the latter material, the animals were functional as well as decorative; they could, for example, be used as bookends.

Acceptance by a fashionable elite, including enthusiastic mention in *Vogue*, along with a measure of financial security encouraged Wright to experiment further with functional objects. Drawing on his experience in fabricating theatrical props, he designed and produced a set of spun pewter bar accessories: bowls, glasses, cocktail shakers. The set was well received, and the Wrights were able to take a lease early in 1931 on a carriage house at 135 East 35th Street.

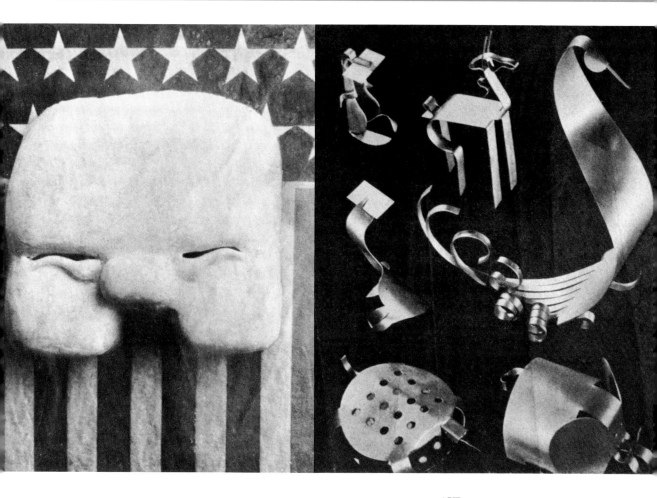

LEFT

4. Herbert Hoover caricature, 1930

Wright's early work designing theatrical sets and props led to his first designs for retail sale: three-dimensional caricatures of celebrities. He used marshmallows for this presidential image, which was published in the first issue of the New Review.

RIGHT

5. Decorative animals, 1930

Hand-cut from sheets of aluminum, these fanciful animals were among Wright's first commercial successes. Like many of the designer's early decorative pieces, they were sold through Rena Rosenthal's well-known shop on Fifth Avenue.

Spun Aluminum

For practical and financial reasons Wright had been forced to rely on outside craftsmen for much of the manufacture of his pewter line. The acquisition of the carriage house made it possible for him to take over many of the manufacturing processes himself. Russel and Mary lived on the upper floor, with the building's other areas devoted to production, shipping, and a sales room.

Wright's original preference for pewter (which he considered a traditional American material) and for chromium-plated steel turned out to be problematical. Both materials required special plating and fabricating machines that were beyond the Wrights' means. It was to counteract these difficulties that he switched to spun aluminum, a far easier material to work than either pewter or steel. By treating the aluminum with emery cloth, he was able to achieve an appearance that closely resembled pewter. With the practical matters of material, immediate expenses, and a workshop resolved, Wright's imagination moved ahead unimpeded. In a short time he had designed and produced the prototypes for an entire line of "informal serving accessories." Later he recalled his admiration for "the easy workability of the metal, its permanent integral coloring." Once settled on material and technique, he found it easy to produce a wide variety of shapes with comparatively little effort.

Wright's bun warmers, cheese servers, ice buckets, "tid-bit trays," "sandwich humidors," beer mugs, pitchers, rarebit dishes, soup tureens, spaghetti sets, and the like were as inventive in their forms as in their functions. Although the shapes had to be at least partially determined by the capabilities of the spinning process, they also reflected Wright's developing preference for rounded and somewhat exaggerated forms. From the start his designs were distinctive, and impossible to confuse with those of other designers, either European or American. His shapes were neither "streamlined" nor Bauhaus-inspired. Despite their conceptual uniqueness and their originality of material and form, Wright's designs were never bizarre. Novel and inventive, yet with no trace of coldness or sterility, they looked modern and fashionably up-to-date. Wright's functional interests were tempered by a relaxed informality: his pieces were intended to be used and enjoyed. Unlike so many modernists, he did not behave during this period as if he were on a moral crusade; one did not have to conscientiously renounce all of one's existing possessions in order to acquire Wright pieces. In fact, the designs were so appealing in concept and form that consumers did not seem to mind that the aluminum was often fashioned with sharp edges, bent with alarming ease, and displayed a disturbing propensity to conduct heat and cold.

Wright's aluminum serving pieces were not only strikingly designed, but they were produced and marketed with unusual sensitivity to the depressed economic and social conditions of the 1930s. While the sheer novelty of the line insured its

OPPOSITE
6. Spun aluminum tea set and "flare vase," early 1930s
Wright designed a line of informal accessories in spun aluminum, and invented the concept of "stove-to-table ware." Popular magazines seized upon Wright's idea of "informal entertaining" which underlay the designs, and Wright was hailed as a harbinger of the future.

**7. Wright brings aluminum out
of the kitchen**
During the 1930s Mary Wright made
frequent public appearances to
demonstrate her husband's spun
aluminum accessories. This sample
table setting is typical of those arranged in department stores and at
trade shows.

OPPOSITE
8. Wright's showroom, ca. 1933
Wright's aluminum "informal serving
accessories" and "stove-to-table
ware" are shown displayed in the
New York showroom he designed.

place in fashionable shops, the wide and enthusiastic press coverage in popular magazines focused on the philosophy of informal entertaining that lay at the heart of the designs. The apparent practicality of the aluminum pieces seemed particularly well suited to contemporary life in homes without household help, where informal family suppers were more common than large formal dinner parties, and where the cocktail party had replaced afternoon tea. Wright was hailed as the harbinger of the future, and his work was associated everywhere with new trends in modern life.

Russel was unmistakably the dominant design force in the partnership, but it is Mary who must be given credit for a good deal of the work's popular success. Her business sense, as well as her New York social connections and financial resources were of vital importance in getting the design business started. Firm in manner and capable of considerable charm, she organized production, planned distribution, and undertook the practical task of selling Russel's work to department and specialty stores. While he attended to his role as designer/craftsman, Mary saw to public relations. She met with magazine editors, made radio and in-store appearances, organized press conferences, and traveled widely, everywhere demonstrating the aluminum serving pieces.

The initial customers for Wright's metal animals and pewter pieces had been wealthy urban sophisticates, and each piece had been hand-made in small numbers for limited distribution in New York specialty shops.[8] Now the aluminum line was being produced in larger quantities for wider distribution. Supported by the concept of "informal living," Wright hoped the new line would appeal to a broad upper middle-class audience. He was attempting not only to retain his early audience, but to open a new market, to attract Americans who were not yet sympathetic to—or even aware of—modern design.

By 1932, Wright's aluminum venture was successful enough for him to engage an outside sales agent, Mary Ryan. Meanwhile, ALCOA introduced a competing line. Wright responded inventively, by expanding his product line at both ends. For his specialty group, he produced one-of-a-kind crystal vases, cylindrical fish tanks, and light spherical vases of vaguely astrological inspiration.[9] He also designed a set of sterling silver flatware along strictly geometric, almost Constructivist, lines. But the greater part of his attention was devoted to the other portion of his business—the informal aluminum pieces. Now he embellished them with cork bases, rattan frames, reed and cane handles, and wooden covers. (Wright was later to describe his perception of aluminum as a "neutral, modest metal" that was an interesting background to other substances.[10]) The combination of warmly colored natural materials with the cool metallic tone of the aluminum was agreeable and distinctive.

Wright then invented the concept of "stove-to-table ware," developing a line of pieces to be used for both cooking and table service. The innovation was particularly well-received in the press. The first designer to adapt what had been a strictly utilitarian material for decorative table use, Wright had "brought aluminum out of the kitchen," according to one account.

He experimented freely, producing everything from bean pots to pretzel baskets and aluminum flower pots. Lamps were made from aluminum tubing, tables and chairs from bent sheet metal. There is a splendid sense of unrestrained fantasy about this early work. As Wright experimented, he gained stylistic assurance. His shapes became more personal and distinctive. Forms tapered more dramatically, spouts and pitcher lips became pronounced. The sleek, highly finished, and machine-made look of the early pewter and chrome pieces was replaced by the far more organic and natural forms that were to characterize Wright's future work.

OPPOSITE
9. Sterling silver flatware, ca. 1933
While concentrating on spun aluminum for a broad market, Wright also produced one-of-a-kind specialty items. This prototype set of silverware was designed under strong European influence.

Early Consulting Work

The success of Wright's aluminum pieces brought with it both a certain celebrity and the chance for professional growth and diversification. In 1931 the Metropolitan Museum of Art invited him to participate in its annual exhibition of Contemporary American Industrial Art, and the following year the Philadelphia Art Museum commissioned an all-aluminum breakfast room for its exhibition, *Machine Art*.[11] This recognition brought Wright his first independent consulting contracts.

The profession of consulting industrial designer was born in the late 1920s and early 1930s of a consumer demand for novelty and an increasing awareness of European design trends. Faced with the saturated markets of the depression, rival manufacturers sought to differentiate their products by "styling," and by using such new marketing concepts as "consumer engineering" and "planned obsolescence."[12] Wright belonged to the pioneering generation of such designers, which included Bel Geddes, Walter Dorwin Teague, Donald Deskey, Raymond Loewy, and Henry Dreyfuss. Although he was a member of this group, Wright was also something of an outsider. Like many of his colleagues, his background was in stage design. But while most of them formed large, highly organized offices that employed a staff of designers working as a team on large-scale products for heavy industry—Dreyfuss designed for ATT, Teague for Kodak, Loewy for the Pennsylvania Railroad—Wright always remained a loner and a craftsman who, despite his occasional work as a design consultant, specialized in household products for his entire career. He stayed aloof from what he regarded as the more superficial aspects of "styling": streamlining, Art Deco, and *moderne*. Unlike many of his colleagues, Wright's first question about a design was never "Will it sell?"

Friends and associates remember him as a man deeply serious about his work and distinctly unwilling to compromise on its aesthetic aspects, even when unreasonably high production costs or functional difficulties might result. His shyness, defensiveness, and stubborn independence made him a difficult partner. Wright saw himself as an artist, not a businessman, and this, too, set him apart from most of his industrial designer colleagues. His personal identification was not with the cool professionals of the New York corporate world, but with the painters, sculptors, and theater people he had met in Woodstock.

Realizing that he had very real limitations as a draftsman, self-conscious about his lack of academic training, and neither verbally facile nor even particularly articulate, Wright learned to exploit his strengths. His response to design challenges was organic and sculptural, sensual rather than visual, intuitive rather than intellectual. He indulged a belief in his own naivete and seemed almost to relish his lack of business acumen. He also resented the time and effort it took to work with a client in a cooperative manner and had little patience for the necessity to create designs that could be produced economically. Wright was always more successful

OPPOSITE
10. Chromium-plated "corn set," mid-1930s
One of Wright's earliest consulting commissions came from the Chase Brass company. This "corn set," 5¼ inches in height, is made of chromium-plated brass.

27

when working on his own. He produced his best designs when he was free to follow his own tastes and instincts. It was at these times that he revealed his paradoxical sensibilities as a man with unique creative powers who was also closely in touch with the public's needs and wants.

The Wurlitzer Company was among Wright's first industrial clients. Late in 1932, it commissioned him to prepare designs for two "midget radios," an accordion, and a modern piano. Wright's Wurlitzer KRW piano was scaled to apartment use and designed for mass production. The instrument was available either in mahogany with copper trim or in ebony and chrome. Sketch books preserved at Dragon Rock attest to how seriously Wright took his commission, and how hard he worked on both the piano's overall form and on its individual details. The legs, keyboard cover, music stand, and trim are blocked out in repeated rectangles of pleasing proportion. The design is not totally successful, however, for the rectilinear forms seem at odds with the curves inherent in a piano's shape. It is interesting to compare Wright's solution to the challenge of designing a modern musical instrument to those arrived at by Walter Dorwin Teague at about the same time.[13] Compared with Teague's design, which employs the conceit of thin chrome rods as legs, Wright's piano looks clean, straightforward, and unmannered. The same adjectives might be applied to Wright's radio designs. His small table-sized receivers were a considerable departure from the large console sets popular during the 1930s. In the directness of their overall design, the sensible control placement, and the avoidance of applied streamlined decoration, they contrast smartly with both the boxy, furniture-sized radios as well as the small, trendier versions designed by his contemporaries.

The early 1930s also brought Wright several interior design commissions. In 1932, he created one of New York's first post-repeal cocktail lounges for the Restaurant Du Relle on Madison Avenue.[14] The lounge featured aluminum stools with cane-wrapped tubular legs, collapsible cork-topped tables, and indirect lighting hidden behind copper wall panels. The overall effect was cool and contemporary.

Perhaps more significant as an indicator for Wright's future development was a chair he designed in 1932 for his own apartment. It was exhibited at the Museum of Modern Art in 1939.[15] Constructed of Primavera wood and covered with pony skin, the handmade chair is an early manifestation of Wright's growing fondness for natural materials and vaguely Surrealist-inspired forms. The chair's soft, biomorphic contours and organically shaped arms are a significant departure from the harder, more mechanical forms of the aluminum tables and chairs that appeared in the Philadelphia exhibition and at the Restaurant Du Relle.

11, 12. Wright modernizes the radio, 1932
Wright's table-sized radios, designed for Wurlitzer, were a significant departure from the large console sets which then dominated the market. Shown here are Wright's 1932 radio (No. 12, bottom) and Wurlitzer's previous model (No. 11, top).

**13. Restaurant Du Relle,
Madison Avenue, 1933**
Wright's early commercial interior designs included one of New York's first post-repeal cocktail lounges.

14. Pony skin chair, 1932
The pony skin and primavera wood chair that Wright designed for his own use reveals the designer's growing fondness for natural materials and organic forms.

Early Furniture Designs

His successful experiment in furniture design persuaded Wright to accept a commission from the Heywood-Wakefield Company of Gardner, Massachusetts to design an entire line of modern furniture. The sixty-piece group was introduced in 1934 at Bloomingdale's department store in New York, displayed in room settings for which Wright designed not only the individual furniture pieces, but the carpets, drapes, lamps, upholstery fabrics, and accessories. The concept of offering for retail sale a coordinated line of furniture and accessories by one designer was a novel one. But Wright's Heywood-Wakefield line was undistinguished: the pieces were almost all boxy in form and heavily upholstered, often with contrasting solid and plaid fabrics used in a single chair. Tables were blocky, with veneered surfaces of contrasting woods. The designs looked familiar and superficially stylish, but they seemed somehow unresolved, not nearly up to the level of the far more interesting aluminum and copper lamps used in the room settings. Some aspects of the line, however, were genuinely original. Instead of designing matching suites of furniture to be purchased as a fixed group and arranged in a specific configuration, Wright stressed flexibility. Each of the pieces and accessories was designed individually, and then coordinated in terms of scale and materials; they could be grouped in any number of ways to suit the needs of the buyer. The "centerpiece" of the line was Wright's design for the first sectional couch—an invention much imitated in subsequent years.

The furniture also presented some difficult technical problems. The Heywood-Wakefield firm, which normally produced traditional colonial furniture in solid woods, had insisted that Wright use veneers, popularly employed in contemporary European furniture, in his designs. When they encountered production difficulties with the veneers Wright had specified, and subsequent delays in delivery, Wright made a counterproposal for a full line of solid maple contemporary furniture. Heywood-Wakefield rejected it, and his contract was not renewed.

Wright's proposed maple furniture, eventually to be produced by the Conant Ball Company, differed in a number of significant ways from his first line for Heywood-Wakefield. For the new line Wright stressed the use of solid native wood in "full, hardy, craftsmanlike forms,"[16] a choice he hoped would both "continue and modernize a century-old tradition of American furniture design."[17] The new pieces were clean, open, functional, and practical in appearance. Less self-consciously stylish than the Heywood-Wakefield line, Wright's maple furniture managed to seem both modern and traditional in appearance. It was also planned to be very reasonably priced, well within the reach of middle-class buyers.

The proposed furniture was basically rectilinear in shape, but edges and corners were rounded or bevelled for softer lines. Wright referred to this as a "cushion

15. Copper torchere lamp, ca. 1934
This lamp was marketed as part of Wright's first furniture line.

NEXT PAGE

16. The coordinated interior, 1934
This sample room was installed in Bloomingdale's Department Store, New York, to launch Wright's line of furniture for the Heywood-Wakefield Company. The idea of making a coordinated line of furniture and accessories available to the general public was a novel one.

17. Modern Living furniture line, 1935
Wright's enormously successful <u>Modern Living</u> furniture was constructed of solid maple and was available in either a reddish tone or, as here, an unstained "blonde" finish.

edge" and considered it as both an aesthetic and practical component of the design. Overall shapes were defined by vertical and horizontal planes, with sheets of wood used in place of conventional legs wherever possible. The pieces were simply constructed out of standard maple lumber, secured at right angles. Mitred corners were avoided in favor of overlapping and butt joints. Upholstery was used sparingly and chair arms were open; though solid and sturdy in construction, the furniture did not appear massive or heavy. The pieces featured hidden storage areas, generous arm rests, and oversized handles for practicality without a loss of style. Working with a severely limited range of materials, Wright achieved a laudable variety within the line. Wright exploited the natural beauty of the maple by offering the line in both a reddish tone and in an unstained natural "blonde" finish—the term coined by Mary Wright to describe its color, which was so much imitated by other designers that it became a cliché of 1930s design.

After the maple line was rejected by Heywood-Wakefield, Wright took his drawings to R.H. Macy and Company in New York. The company's enthusiastic response secured Wright a production contract with the Conant Ball Company of Gardner, Massachusetts. The line was launched with a major national promotion in the fall of 1935, culminating in the opening of an entire nine-room "Modern Maple House" at Macy's Herald Square store. Virtually every item in the displays was designed by Wright.

While such totally designed rooms were commonplace in custom interiors, Wright's were the first to be offered on a mass-market basis. The entire *Modern Living* package presented by Macy's was extraordinarily successful. In its unaffected simplicity and lack of artifice, the line contrasted dramatically with the furniture being designed by Walter Dorwin Teague, Paul Frankl, John Vassos, and Joseph Urban. Even the work of Gilbert Rohde, whose career in many ways seems to parallel Wright's, seems pretentious when compared to the Macy's pieces. Wright's work is decidedly populist in tone, appealingly unostentatious in its avoidance of the precious materials and sleek finishes favored by his contemporaries. Indeed, the Conant Ball line, with its clean modernity, might well be a healthy urban descendant of turn-of-the-century mission-style furntiture. It was, after all, mission furniture which had filled Wright's boyhood home; he was to recall it fondly later as an important source of his inspiration.

In planning the advertising for the *Modern Living* line, Wright drew skillfully on his theater experience to convey the sense of total environment that was implicit in the Modern Maple House. While he used such calculated sales points as practicality and good value, American design and manufacture, and modernity with respect for tradition, he also recognized the need for a star attraction for the printed advertisements. He convinced Macy's to abandon its usual policy and use his name in all advertising.[18] This promotional method not only successfully introduced a line of furniture, but for the first time made Wright's name known to a nationwide audience.

Wright had judged the practical needs as well as the psychological mood of the public with great accuracy. In the middle of the depression, he provided a line that looked unmistakably modern, yet was visibly and reassuringly a part of a long American tradition of solid wood furniture. The *Modern Living* line, produced by Conant Ball and displayed at Macy's, is the first group of work in which Wright reveals himself to be a fully formed and mature designer with his own identifiable style. He was now clearly in possession of a coherent and distinctive aesthetic vision, one that would govern the rest of his career.

American Modern Dinnerware

While Mary Wright's promotional talents and shrewd business sense were important factors in Russel's early success, the designer/businessman Irving Richards was an equally powerful influence on his mature work. Acknowledging their shared interests and complementary skills, Wright and Richards pooled their capital and formed a partnership, Russel Wright Associates, late in 1935. Wright was to handle most of the design work, while Richards looked after manufacturing and distribution: Mary became a director of the new corporation. This arrangement left Wright free to pursue outside consulting jobs. Richards encouraged Wright to develop a personal style based on the model of the Conant Ball furniture. He also insisted on better quality control in the designs the new company undertook to manufacture. The spun aluminumware, somewhat flimsy in its original version, was redesigned in a heavier grade. Together Wright and Richards put together an illustrated sales catalogue of accessories and lamps and increased the efficiency of distribution procedures. Recognizing where the greatest commercial potential lay, Richards directed Wright away from the hand-production of small decorative pieces toward simple, inventive designs that could be mass-produced for a broad middle-class audience. Wright had always felt awkward and ill at ease with the urban socialites who bought his early work. Now his midwestern Quaker roots, and perhaps some guilt at having disappointed his family's expectations, were supporting the increasing sense of social consciousness he was feeling in his design work. By the time he and Richards became partners, Wright was eager to produce designs that mattered socially as well as aesthetically.

Around 1937, he began to shift his attention from furniture design to ceramics. With his creation of *American Modern* dinnerware, he produced what was to become his greatest artistic and commercial success. The *American Modern* pieces were simply and organically molded in soft, rimless forms and were glazed with unusual, mottled colors—Seafoam Blue, Granite Grey, Chartreuse Curry, Bean Brown.[19]

In both shape and color the line was without stylistic precedent. In designing *American Modern*, Wright had called on his craftsman's ability to allow his designs' basic shapes to grow out of their intended use. At the same time, a sculptor's responsiveness to abstract form is clearly at work in the pieces. While he never allows functional considerations to overwhelm aesthetic ones, his own particular blend of the two is wholly original and curiously timeless. Neither Art Deco, nor *moderne*, nor streamlined, the pieces escape any conventional stylistic or historical label.

Though Wright was very reticent about expressing interest in the work of others, certain formal influences can be detected. The flowing lines, folded lips, and exaggerated spouts of many *American Modern* pieces must have been designed

OPPOSITE

18. American Modern water pitcher, designed 1937
This piece is among the most distinctive and sculptural in the line. American Modern dinnerware was produced by Steubenville Pottery from 1939 to 1959.

with at least a general admiration for the contemporary European Surrealist movement, and particularly for the sculpture of Jean Arp.[20] Unlike most Surrealist work, however, Wright's forms are not emotionally demanding or intrusive. Instead, they suggest a soft, vaguely organic sexuality that is reassuring rather than ominous or hostile. Wright also seems to have adopted some traditional non-ceramic forms in his designs. The *American Modern* water pitcher, for example, is strikingly similar to a classic American coal scuttle, while the set's soup bowls are variations on the eighteenth-century porringer.

The colors of the pieces are even more distinctive than their shapes. While Wright's "palette" is arresting, the shades he chooses are not gay or obvious like those of the popular contemporary *Fiestaware*. Wright arrived at his color combinations only after much experimentation. By using a mottled underglaze, he lowered the key of his colors and muted them with underlying grays, so that they are at once saturated and restrained, sensual and elusive. He worked with ceramic engineers at Alfred University on these unusual glazes and succeeded in developing colors that were individually distinctive but that could also be used in mixed combinations: Seafoam cups with Granite saucers, Coral with Brown.

When the dinnerware line was introduced in stores, Wright prepared a slide lecture to illustrate the ideas it embodied. Tableware should, he pronounced, "dramatize" food service. Designs should form a visually flattering background for food and should simultaneously establish a mood for the meal. All the elements of the environment—table setting, glassware, linens, lamps, flowers—must be considered and coordinated. While such ideas reflected established practice in the Orient, they were revolutionary in the America of the 1930s.

Wright believed that successful dinnerware designs should not be hard and mechanical in appearance, but soft and warm, simple and geometric in shape without sharp angles. Patterned decoration was distracting, and the color white, anathema: it made food look dead and opaque. For his soft, slightly mottled, glazes, Wright especially favored black, brown, and middle gray as colors which provided maximum visual impact for food.

The designs for *American Modern* were essentially complete in 1937, but the dinnerware constituted such a departure from accepted aesthetic norms that no manufacturer felt it would sell. It took Wright nearly three years and a considerable financial outlay to find a factory willing to undertake production. Finally, the bankrupt Steubenville Pottery in East Liverpool, Ohio was convinced to take the gamble, and the first dinnerware reached the stores late in 1939.

19. American Modern "stack server" and "covered casserole"
These designs are typical of Wright's penchant for space- and labor-saving shapes.

NEXT PAGE
20. American Modern, produced 1939-1959
Shown here are (clockwise from lower left): American Modern cream pitcher, cup and saucer, teapot, salt and pepper, and celery dish.

AMERICAN
MODERN dinnerware
designed by *Russel Wright*
• 29 LOVELY PIECES TO CHOOSE FROM • 6 DELIGHTFUL COLORS

Now you can collect a set of America's most inviting dinnerware
—tailored to your own taste. American Modern offers a variety of
shapes and sizes that will meet every service requirement...in
harmonizing colors (as shown on the cover) you can combine to bring
new beauty to your table: White, Coral, Cedar Green, Granite
Grey, Chartreuse Curry and Black Chutney.

21. American Modern brochure, 1950s
More than any other single set of designs, it was American Modern dinnerware that made Wright's name a household word in the 1940s and 1950s.

22. The "starter set"
The dinnerware "starter set" was a Wright invention. Consumers were offered inexpensive basic place settings in the hope that they would later commit themselves to a full line of more expensive serving pieces. This package holds a "starter set" of Residential, a plastic dinnerware Wright designed in 1953.

The line's strong personality seemed to discourage store china buyers and to enrage critics. Prototypes commissioned by Wright sold well in specialty shops, but the larger stores were unconvinced. The reaction of Manny Farber of the *New Republic*, who complained of finding in *American Modern* a "quality of steeliness," a "nudity," and a "hammerlike statement and chi-chi color," was not unusual.[21] In spite of Wright's attempts to avoid such stereotypical characteristics of the modern as hardness and coldness, these are the very qualities critics saw in the designs. And Emily Post attacked the very idea of informal service—in several letters to *Time*, which Wright answered with great gusto.[22] Ironically, Post had been an admirer of Wright's early pewter and chromium pieces. By far the best indication of Wright's abandonment by his first customers came in a note in the *New Yorker's* "On and Off the Avenue" column, a space in which his early work had been highly praised:

> *If the fervent reception of the pottery of Russel Wright…did nothing else, it demonstrated that the passionate desire for color and new forms on the part of our citizens was such that they were evidently ready to swallow a large helping of eccentricity and some vulgarity in their appetite for modern crockery. Mr. Wright's success may thus have served to persuade designers and potters with more talent but less business acumen that the production of earthenware with a contemporary feeling would be a shrewd venture…[23]*

Undaunted, Wright made personal calls on the retail stores' unwilling china buyers, paid for newspaper ads himself, offered to take back all stock that remained unsold, and once again drew upon his theater background to build a public for *American Modern*. The dinnerware was literally promoted like a Broadway show. Advertisements stressed that *American Modern* was planned to complement "the unique informality of modern American life" —the theme, first developed for the Conant Ball furniture, to which Wright was to return repeatedly throughout his life. He gave radio interviews, made personal appearances in stores, wrote articles for women's magazines, and presented his slide lecture to women's clubs. He invented the concept of the "starter set," an ingenious idea that made sixteen pieces of the dinnerware available to buyers at near-production cost. It was hoped that, once committed to the line, shoppers would return to purchase the more expensive service pieces.

And return they did. Within two years the factory was unable to keep up with the demand. More than eighty million pieces of *American Modern* were ultimately produced over the next twenty years, making it the most popular mass-produced

23. Commercial interior design, 1939
Wright designed this showroom for the International Handkerchief Company like an assembly line. Customers were moved efficiently through a series of moulded flowing spaces from entrance to displays to exit.

OPPOSITE
24. 1939 World's Fair exhibit
Wright's design for the "Focal Foods" display at the 1939 New York World's Fair was among his most clearly surrealist. Visitors peered at the exhibits through large biomorphic openings in the wall.

pattern ever sold. At one point during 1940, demand for it was so great that a two-by-four inch newspaper advertisement announcing the arrival of a shipment at Gimbel's New York store produced block-long lines and near-riot.[24] Customers did not seem to mind that *American Modern*, made of soft pottery clay, broke with alarming ease, that the crevices and overhanging lips were remarkably difficult to wash, or that some of the shapes were oddly unsuited to their stated purpose—the neck of the water pitcher, for example, was too narrow to receive ice cubes, and the sugar bowl defied efforts to remove its contents.

In 1939 Wright also undertook two important interior design projects. The New York showroom he designed for the International Handkerchief Company[25] is an organic "assembly line" of diagonally interconnected spaces and flowingly curved walls. Potential customers are moved efficiently from the door to the reception desk, then on to waiting areas, displays, sales rooms, and even a bar. The displays, in rectangular and circular wall cases, were surrealist in inspiration and created a strong contrast with the cool, uniform tones of the surrounding room. Actual sales areas were curtained for privacy and featured slant-topped tables and special lighting to dramatize the contents of the company's sample books. Each individual handkerchief was displayed in these books against a colored background designed to show it to its best advantage.

Wright's rejection of what he called a "T-square and compass"[26] approach to design, in favor of more organic and surrealist-inspired forms, found its most unusual expression in the exhibitions that he designed for the 1939 New York World's Fair. In the largest of these, the focal foods exhibition, the visitor moved through dark halls where biomorphically shaped openings cut in walls revealed dioramas that depicted food production and distribution, including a field that could smile or scowl and a group of flying lobsters.

**25,26. Wright's American Way,
1940**
The American Way, a cooperative
marketing program involving sixty-
five artists, craftsmen, and manufacturers, was launched at Macy's
New York store.

The American Way

As his design schemes became more and more successful, Wright displayed a tendency for needlessly complicating his professional affairs. Uncomfortable and insecure in business dealings, he was suspicious of any arrangement that seemed too simple. His relationships with clients, even when governed by tightly drawn contracts, were often punctuated by acrimonious letters and all too often ended in law suits. Wright seemed sincere in wanting to absent himself from business activities, but time and again he could not bring himself to relinquish control.

His temperament was displayed with particular clarity when he and Irving Richards dissolved their partnership. Wright and Richards had formed Russel Wright Associates in 1935. Almost immediately, Wright initiated a series of reorganizations designed to free him from everyday involvement with the business. In 1939, just as *American Modern* dinnerware was becoming established, he sold out his holdings to Richards. Only later was Wright to realize how dearly he had paid for his freedom in terms of the reduced income he received from sales of *American Modern*.[27]

This freedom, after ten years of day-to-day involvement with his business, came as a great relief; to celebrate it, Wright embarked on an extended cross-country trip. It was during the course of this vacation that he contrived to re-enter the business world he had just left. With Richards' advice, he conceived of a plan to market a complete line of home furnishings designed and produced by a cooperative of sixty-five artists, craftsmen, and manufacturers. The line was to be sold through major department stores and promoted under the name *American Way*. At the heart of Wright's concept, which he later came to regard as exaggeratedly idealistic and chauvinistic, was a desire to overcome what he saw as America's cultural inferiority complex, a mission he would accomplish by demonstrating the quality and vitality of American design.

The theme of a national inferiority complex became a frequent one for Wright during these years. His cross-country trip, his midwestern roots, the realities of the depression, his personal rejection of contemporary European design, and the threat of war all contributed to his perspective. In magazine articles and speeches, he condemned American educators for preaching the superiority of European art.[28] He praised national diversity and exhorted audiences to discover and celebrate America's beautiful landscape, its abundant resources, and its rich heritage. He wrote lyrically about such characteristic pieces of Americana as the skyscraper, about "our shining bathrooms and efficient kitchens," "our gleaming fat automobiles," "our gas stations and movie palaces."[29]

Wright's vision of art and life had other aspects: he wanted to banish the stereotype of the artist as a "nineteenth century garret aesthete" and then, through the medium of modern industrial design, to make Americans more aware both of their immediate surroundings and of all aspects of the visual world. It was this developing philosophy that eventually led to his decision during the 1960s to work for the United States Parks Service, and later, to open his home, Dragon Rock, to the public.

n 1940, however, these plans were still far in the future, and Wright was fully occupied with the *American Way* project. He drew up a list of specific objectives, which included fostering "expression in handicraft work of our picturesque regional life" and developing U.S.-made household products of "inherently American design" for both mass and craft production.[30] The *American Way* would deter the prevailing "forced adherence to past periods or the abrupt introduction of unprecedented ideas." It was American designers, Wright contended, who knew American needs, and it is they who could best tailor merchandise to our way of life.

Together with a small staff, Wright traveled the country selecting objects for the *American Way* line and negotiating manufacturing contracts. He recruited a distinguished board of directors, which included Edgar Kaufmann, Jr., architects John W. Root and Edward Durrell Stone, designer and advertising man Egmont Arens, his old Martha's Vineyard employer, painter Boardman Robinson, and Macy's vice-president Edwin I. Marks. He also enlisted the cooperation of the designers Raymond Loewy, Walter Dorwin Teague, and Gilbert Rohde, who agreed to make certain of their designs available to the project. Always aware of prevailing popular taste, Wright convinced John Steuart Curry and Grant Wood to provide designs for textiles and framed reproductions of their work. Naturally, Wright's own Steubenville dinnerware and aluminum accessories were also included, as well as some new furniture designs, manufactured by the Monitor and the Sprague and Carleton companies. The entire line was priced to appeal to buyers with a family income between $2,000 and $5,000.

Once selected and distributed, merchandise was displayed in department store model rooms, much as had been done for Wright's Heywood-Wakefield and Conant Ball furniture lines. Again the emphasis was not on "a forced matching of exact design types," but on "a feeling for harmonious design relationships and color combinations." The model rooms were presented only as guides, as examples of the kind of combinations that could be achieved. Consumers were encouraged to assemble rooms that expressed their own particular needs. The aim was, in Wright's words, to provide "unity with freedom to make our own choice—the American Way!" The phrase was not yet laden with the aura of fervent anti-communism that would come to characterize such slogans after the war.

Aware of consumer resistance to what was perceived as the cold, hard, and

27. Dragon Rock, completed 1961

Dragon Rock, Wright's home near Garrison, New York, was the culmination of the designer's career. Shown here is part of the living room (foreground), with cushions on rocks for seating; below is the dining room. The floors are natural slate, and an uncut cedar tree supports the ceiling. Drapes, slipcovers, and rugs were changed to best complement the changing landscape visible through huge two-story windows. Warm reds and browns predominated during winter months.

28. American Way publicity, 1940

First Lady Eleanor Roosevelt opened the initial American Way displays at Macy's.

29. Machine-made ceramics, 1945-46
Although mass-produced in standard shapes and colors, Wright's designs for the Bauer Pottery Company simulate the appearance of hand-made art pottery.

mechanical character of modern design, Wright stressed the functional and traditional character of *American Way* products. A close observer of the American regional consciousness and of its popular resurgence, he arranged his products by geographic area—a "veritable travelogue of crafts." Wright had a special sensitivity to the fact that most Americans felt insecure about aesthetic matters, and his model rooms and "pre-chosen" lines of merchandise assisted shy consumers in putting together interiors that were personal and expressive, but still reassuringly within the bounds of accepted taste. Furthermore, the price range of *American Way* goods gave the program a decidedly populist flavor. Wright also took advantage of the growing American suspicion of all things European: the *American Way* was an avowedly nationalist program. (He even managed to arrange for First Lady Eleanor Roosevelt to cut the ribbon at the *American Way* display at Macy's New York store![31])

While the program designs categorically rejected the aesthetics of the German Bauhaus, which Wright had greatly admired early in his career, it paradoxically and not altogether coincidentally shared certain social aims with the German enterprise. Gropius and his colleagues had worked to unite the fine and applied arts, to reconcile traditional crafts with machine production, and to blend practical and theoretical knowledge. Wright's goals were similar. He further extended the design and manufacturing emphasis of the Bauhaus to the point where distribution took place. Just as the Bauhaus was a quintessentially European phenomenon, founded on utopian ideas with long English and Continental pedigrees, so the *American Way*, in its mixture of romantic, nationalist, populist, and capitalist elements, was peculiarly American.

But there the comparison must end. While Wright offered products at low prices, he was never able to reconcile the very different practical demands and aesthetic qualities of hand- and machine-produced designs. In the *American Way* program, the two means of merchandise production were strictly separated, and the quality of both was very uneven. Even the best products Wright and his associates offered did not reach the level of Bauhaus quality.

Two sets of Wright designs show the aesthetic problem that afflicted much *American Way* merchandise. For the Klise Woodenware Company of Grand Rapids, Michigan, Wright fashioned a set of free-form wooden serving pieces. The line, dubbed *Oceana*, was entirely machine-produced, but simulated the appearance of hand-carved work. He took a similar approach in a group of designs for machine-made ceramics commissioned by the Bauer Pottery Company.[32] Both the ceramics and the woodenware, although not unattractive, are curiously schizophrenic designs that seem to emit eerily mixed messages. A cursory inspection of both leaves us with the impression that they were made by hand, but closer observation reveals the pieces to be disturbingly mechanical in appearance. Aesthetic decisions about grain in the wood or glazing seem to have been arbitrary, and in general the designs lack both the clarity and the fully resolved character of the best of Wright's earlier work.

The *American Way* program opened with considerable fanfare and wide press coverage, combined with acres of advertising.[33] Public reaction was encouraging at first, but practical difficulties soon developed. Logistics were a problem; it proved almost impossible to coordinate deliveries from sixty-five suppliers, many of whom were quite small. Shortages quickly developed, with disappointed consumers in their wake. Quality control was also difficult, and Wright tried to bolster the line by forming a nine-man jury to revise selection and upgrade the level of the crafts. All furniture was redesigned with a single finish for added unity. But neither these measures nor others were very successful. Supply and distribution problems persisted, soon aggravated by wartime shortages. Wright, intensely disappointed, was forced to liquidate the *American Way* in 1942.[34] The program, despite all his hopes for it, did not in the end rise above the level of an elaborate sales scheme.

Easier Living

Exempted from active military service because of poor eyesight and his age, Wright spent most of the war working for the Red Cross and conducting extensive independent surveys of food service methods and housekeeping techniques. These studies provided the basic themes for Russel and Mary Wright's book, the *Guide to Easier Living*, which was published in 1950.[35]

In *Easier Living*, the Wrights contend that traditional concepts of what constitutes "gracious living" are a sham. Comfort, ease, and spontaneity are frequently sacrificed to outmoded dreams of life with numerous servants. Instead, modern American homes must be designed to better express ideas of democracy and individualism. The Wrights also struck a blow for equality of the sexes by asserting that housework need not be demeaning for either men or women. *Easier Living* is a blend of manifesto and helpful hints. In chapters with such titles as "Home Sweet Home," "Room to Relax," "The Vanishing Dining Room," "The Housewife Engineer," and "The New Hospitality," the Wrights offer a variety of functional advice. Much of it is obvious:

> develop routines for chores…involve the whole family in cooking and cleaning…space out cleaning to different days…cut down on dish washing with one-dish meals…add casters to furniture for easier moving…ask your guests to help with party cleanup

Some is more daring:

> drastically reduce the number of your possessions to make maintenance easier…replace sit-down meals with "family cafeteria" service …use only throwaway paper plates for most meals…redecorate your home, replacing old fashioned fabrics and surfaces with easy-care plastics

The *New Yorker* summed up the book in a way that still seems fair today:

> It is doubtful whether the new life [proposed by the Wrights] differs very much—except in being more self-conscious and less pleasing—from that led by most young Americans of the present day. The best part of the book is a series of drawings and specifications for magnificent closets and other storage spaces…It is in the sections devoted to entertaining and household management that the value of the work… is most debatable. In connection with party-giving, the "work-saving" idea as applied to food and service is pursued so relentlessly that one can't help wondering why it was not carried to its logical conclusion: no party at all. Under household management, the modern ways of doing things advocated by the Wrights (when both hands are full, use your elbow to close the refrigerator door) may make many readers wonder if they haven't, quite unconsciously, been leading the easy life all along.[36]

OPPOSITE

30, 31. American Modern dinnerware, designed 1937
ABOVE: coffee, tea, and "after dinner" pots were designed with extended spouts and flowing organic lines. BELOW: a place setting. Wright encouraged customers to mix colors in a single setting of American Modern.

Later Ceramic Designs

The book reflects the major change that had taken place in Wright's professional outlook. The optimism and unrestrained creative excitement that distinguished his early work and writings had been replaced by the late 1940s, with a certain rigidity and coldness, a preoccupation with function.

By the mid-1940s Wright had expanded his business to include lines of glassware, flatware, and table linens, all designed to accompany *American Modern* dinnerware. (As he had sold the line's production rights to Irving Richards, he was earning only royalty income from the ceramics.) He designed a set of colored glassware for the Morgantown Glass Guild in shades and forms coordinated with the dinnerware. The table linens, made by a number of different manufacturers, soon followed. And in 1951 the John Hull Company introduced an unusual line of Russel Wright stainless flatware. All the pieces, including the knife, were machine stamped from sheet stock. The glassware, linens, and flatware were all marketed under the *American Modern* label, with Wright's name prominently displayed as designer.

Following the success of these lines, in 1949 Wright designed a set of tumblers for the Imperial Glass Company. Dubbed *Flair*, the emphatically shaped glasses were available in clear, colored, and "seed" glass. Wright was the first to use the heavily textured seed glass for table service. The following year he introduced a line of monochromatic plaid and checked tablecloths, which competed successfully with the pastel damask and lace cloths that then dominated the market. The tablecloths were followed in quick succession by table mats and a group of printed tablecloths.

During these same years Wright also expanded his dinnerware production by entering market areas that were not being supplied by *American Modern*.[37] In 1948 he created a line of vitreous china for hotel and restaurant use, produced by the Sterling China Company. The heavy-bodied pieces were designed for hard service and are consequently less freely shaped than those in the domestic *American Modern* line. Cup and pitcher handles are aligned with the rims of the vessels and conform to the overall shapes of the pieces. To further reduce the possibility of breakage, projecting knobs were replaced by grips that were moulded into the piece. The restaurant line was produced in Straw Yellow, Suede Grey, Cedar Brown, and in a handsome Ivy Green. Custom pieces with painted decoration were also produced. Unfortunately, it proved difficult to achieve consistency in the glazes, and the line was not widely accepted.

Far more popular was Wright's *Casual China* designed in the same spirit of the restaurant dinnerware but for home use. Produced by the Iroquois China Company of Syracuse, New York and initially distributed by Garrison Products of New York City, the line stands formally midway between *American Modern* and

OPPOSITE
32. American Modern pitchers and gravy boat
In designing American Modern, Wright worked as both a sculptor and a craftsman, balancing aesthetics and functional utility against each other.

NEXT PAGE
33. American Modern glassware, 1951
Wright designed a set of table glasses in shapes and colors to complement his American Modern dinnerware.

the restaurant ware produced for Sterling. Glazes were smoother and less mottled, and the shapes were generally less exaggerated than in the commercial line. Certain pieces were wonderfully inventive, such as the wine carafe, with its extended neck/handle, and the stacking sugar-creamer and salt-pepper combinations. The "pinch" grips and heavy high-fired china body of the Sterling line were also used in these new designs.[38]

While *Casual China* remains one of Wright's most pleasing designs, in the 1940s and 50s its most significant selling point was its durability. Some critics had faulted *American Modern* for its fragility; Wright offered starter sets of *Casual China* with a full replacement guarantee against chipping and breakage in normal use—underwritten by the Mercantile Insurance Company. To safeguard his investment, he designed the line in heavy, solid forms for easy stacking during storage and for resistance to damage during washing and use.[39] Because it was a true china rather than a softer-based stoneware or pottery, *Casual China* was also suitable for "stove-to-table" use.

The line sold well, but in 1950 Wright would redesign most of the serving pieces for a more elegant appearance. The new shapes were less distinctive and more self-consciously sophisticated in form. Traditional knobs replaced the depressed "pinch" grips, and the overall weight of the pieces was significantly lessened.

In 1951, Wright added yet another line: *Highlight* dinnerware, made by the Paden City (West Virginia) Pottery and marketed in New York by Justin Tharaud. The novelty of this line lay in the combined use of pottery and white-flecked snowglass in the same setting.[40] Ceramic cups were matched with glass saucers, and ceramic serving dishes and soup plates came with glass covers. There was also a matching line of drinking glasses in the same two materials. The shapes resembled those used in the Sterling line, except that each piece was rimmed with a thin white highlight.

RIGHT
34. Restaurant china, 1948
Wright's line for Sterling China, intended for hotel and restaurant use, was solid in construction and functional in design.

OPPOSITE
35. Casual China, 1946
Shown here are the butter dish, mug, divided plate, and stacking salt and pepper shakers. The cream pitcher, lower right, is one of several pieces Wright redesigned in 1951 in more self-consciously "elegant" shapes.

While he was at work on these ceramic lines, Wright retained the same
enthusiasm for new and innovative materials that had led him years
before to experiment with spun aluminum. In 1945 he had been approached by American Cyanamid to design a set of dinnerware using the recently
developed thermo-plastic, Melamine. It took American Cyanamid four years to
find a manufacturer for Wright's prototypes. In 1949 General American Transportation brought out the line under the name *Meladur*. The Wright designs were
far more refined in shape, solid in construction, and saturated in color than the
flimsy, ill-conceived, throwaway dishes that were first made with Melamine.
Similar claims can be made for his other designs, *Residential* (1953) and *Flair*
(1959), produced in the same material by Northern Industrial Chemical
of Boston.[41]

All of Wright's plastic pieces reflect their moulded construction. In contrast to
traditional ceramic forms, derived from wheel throwing, the *Residential* pieces
have no central axis and few geometric curves. The moulded plates and bowls
flow organically into integral grips and handles. Design journals praised Wright
for the clever manner in which he concealed mould lines on the completed pieces.
(In 1955, he also designed a line of polyethylene dinnerware for the Ideal Toy
Company and a matching line of toy-sized reproductions of *American Modern* for
children.) His plastic designs enjoyed great popularity in the food service industry,
and, because they combined elegance and sophistication with their solid construction, plastic dinnerware also became for the first time a plausible aesthetic option
for home use.

Designs of the Fifties

None of Wright's designs for china or plastic equalled the phenomenal success of *American Modern*, and by 1950 the unpleasant memory of the *American Way* failure had faded sufficiently to permit Wright to organize another major marketing program. The publication of *Easier Living* was an auspicious moment to launch a coordinated line of merchandise that reflected the principles the Wrights outlined in the book. The cornerstone of the line was a group of fifty pieces of furniture, produced by the Statton Furniture Company of Hagerstown, Maryland. These clean and unmannered pieces are among Wright's best designs. Made of solid, natural-finished sycamore, they are crisper and lighter in appearance than his earlier furniture, with sharper corners and edges and generally less organic forms. Hinges, as well as lapped and pegged joints, are exposed for decorative advantage.[42]

The Statton furniture incorporates many of the kinds of practical gimmicks suggested in *Easier Living*. The lounge chair, for example, has one arm that folds up to provide a broad writing surface, while the other opens into a self-contained magazine rack. A coffee table has a sliding top that opens to reveal an inset porcelain tray to hold food and beverages. Beds have tilting headboards that conceal storage compartments; they also prop open to provide support for reading. A magazine stand is set on casters for easy movement from room to room. Slipcovers snap on and off for easy cleaning, and a nighttable has pull-out shelves which can extend over the bed for eating or reading.[43] As a part of the same line, Wright also offered a coordinated series of lamps, rugs, drapes, and upholstery.

Although it was moderately priced and critically well received, the Statton furniture line did not live up to the expectations of either its designer or its manufacurer. One reason for its lack of commercial success may have been that, given the unusual solidity of Wright's earlier designs, these 1950 pieces seem both flimsy

OPPOSITE
38. Modern Living furniture, 1935
Wright's solid maple furniture blended modernism and tradition. The line was Wright's first great popular success. A night table is shown here (with American Modern ceramics and napkin).

BELOW
39. Easier Living armchair, 1950
The Easier Living furniture line was inspired by Russel and Mary Wright's book of the same name. A number of labor-saving innovations were included in each piece. Here, one chair arm folds up to provide a writing surface while the other opens to reveal a self-enclosed magazine rack.

and somewhat institutional in comparison. They also seemed to lack Wright's own very particular signatures of friendliness and whimsey. Wright had somehow lost touch with the public mood. With the war safely behind them, American consumers now preferred furnishings that expressed conventional prosperity, conformity, and tradition. The modern designs that did manage to succeed in this climate possessed qualities of aesthetic compromise that Wright now seemed unable, or unwilling, to provide.

n contrast to the almost unbroken string of successes which characterized his work of the 1930s, Wright's comparative failures during the forties and fifties were an enormous disappointment to him. In a 1976 speech to the Society of Industrial Designers, which he had served as an activist president in the early fifties, he recalled his mood at this time:

> About 1953, "comtemporary" began to be defeated. My religion, which I had pioneered for twenty years, was losing. I wanted to convert the masses—to design for middle and lower-class Americans a way of life expressive of what I thought was basic American taste. Now with postwar affluence…Easier Living, my book and design group… have failed.[44]

Mary died of cancer in 1952, a terrible loss. Without her to urge him on, without Irving Richards to aid with organization and sales, and without public successes to bolster his always precarious self-esteem, Wright retreated more and more into isolation. In 1941 the Wrights had purchased an eighty-acre tract of land overlooking the Hudson River near Garrison, New York. After Mary died, Wright withdrew from his New York City design practice and increasingly spent his time at Dragon Rock, as he had christened the property.

Wright's withdrawal from business was neither total nor immediate. During the later 1950s and early 1960s, he attempted in a variety of ways to adapt to the times. Ironically, the decline of his design practice coincided with the period of his greatest recognition by the design profession. Between 1950 and 1955, his work was regularly included in the *Good Design* exhibitions which Edgar Kaufmann, Jr. organized for the Museum of Modern Art.[45] In 1950 and 1951 he was represented in the Society of Industrial Designers' annual exhibitions, in 1951 in the Museum of Modern Art's *Design for U.S.A.*, and in two shows mounted by the Albright-Knox Art Gallery in Buffalo: *Good Design is Your Business* (1947) and *Twentieth Century Design: U.S.A.* (1959). He was elected President of the American Society of Industrial Designers in 1952.[47] In 1959, a poll of designers and laymen published in *Fortune* magazine selected *American Modern* dinnerware as twenty-second of the "100 Best-Designed Products."[48]

OPPOSITE
40. Metal folding chair and table, 1950
During the 1950s there was a great surge in the popularity of porch and patio entertaining—an aspect of the informal American lifestyle that Wright championed. Wright's designs for folding furniture for indoor and outdoor use are unusually solid, attractive, and comfortable.

NEXT PAGE
41. American Modern flatware, Highlight china, 1951
All the pieces in Wright's American Modern flatware were stamped from single sheets of stainless steel. The tablecloth and Highlight china are also Wright designs of 1951.

The publicity and prestige generated by these activities and by Wright's frequent lecture tours of design schools and college campuses made it possible for him to secure design commissions in what were for him untried areas. In 1955 Shwayder Brothers commissioned several pieces of folding metal outdoor furniture to be marketed under their Samsonite label. Wright's chairs were available in either bent plywood or with painted and moulded aluminum seats in aqua, coral, chartreuse, and green. There was also a table in matching colors. Five years later, the success of the Samsonite pieces led Shwayder to commission a line of school furniture. Wright was attracted by the social aspects of the commission and applied himself with great enthusiasm. He visited schools, talked with educators, and, characteristically, collected an unusual quantity of background data. His purpose was to produce a friendly, lively environment for school children, with sturdy, comfortable, and easily movable furniture. The line was designed in steel tubing with plywood and reinforced plastic writing surfaces. Each piece stood on ball-in-socket glides. The most innovative aspect of the line was its use of color.[49] Instead of the traditional gray specified for all school furnishings since the early 1930s, the Wright versions offered a choice of four separate, subdued shades.

Still casting about for new challenges, Wright accepted a commission from Du Pont to select colors and design patterns for a line of vinyl upholstery fabrics. In 1952, General Electric hired him to design a ceramic-faced wall clock, and three years later he tried his hand at commercial package design. In that year he also fashioned a decanter and box for Calvert Reserve Whiskey. A reusable jar for Big Top Peanut Butter followed in 1959, a catsup bottle for Hunt Foods in 1960, and a new label and bottle shape for Cresca Foods in 1961.

Until the 1950s, all of Wright's ceramic designs had avoided applied decoration as a strict matter of principle.[50] But in 1951, with his *White Clover* pattern for the Harker Pottery Company, and later with the *Esquire Collection* (1956) for Edwin Knowles, he now bowed to what he perceived as prevailing taste and added applied floral patterns to his dishes.[51] The specific motifs that Wright used for these lines—and, indeed, much of his new sympathy for naturalistic decoration—can be traced to his increasing involvement with the landscaping of Dragon Rock.[52] Still, his willingness to accommodate popular taste, rather than strive to shape it, reflects his lack of direction and the disillusionment he felt during these years.

OPPOSITE ABOVE
42. White Clover dinnerware, 1951
Early in his career Wright had been adamant in his opposition to applied decoration on dinnerware. By 1951, when he designed this pattern for Harker Pottery, he had become more flexible.

OPPOSITE BELOW
43. School furniture, 1955
Wright's Samsonite folding chair was successful enough for the company to commission a second group of furniture from him five years later. The designer's line of school furniture was innovative for its use of color—banned previously as distracting to student attention.

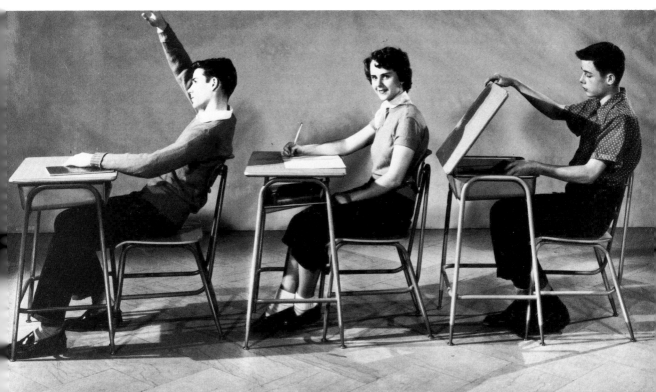

Dragon Rock

In flagging spirits, Wright was beginning to disengage himself from his design practice altogether when in 1955 a catalyst appeared from an unexpected source, renewing his sense of purpose. He was approached by the International Cooperation Administration of the U.S. State Department, and invited to survey the handicraft industries of Southeast Asia in order to recommend strategies for effective American aid in that war-devastated region. For two months, Wright toured Japan, Hong Kong, Thailand, Vietnam, Cambodia, and Taiwan, conducting his survey and exploring possibilities for international trade.

Although the trip was physically taxing and beset with bureaucratic red tape, it was a great success in a number of ways. The report that Wright prepared for the State Department after his return was widely circulated and praised, and apparently had some influence in changing American preconceptions about the essential nature of the handicraft culture in Southeast Asia.[53] The large exhibition of material he gathered in the East, which Wright mounted in 1956 at the International Housewares Show in New York, secured for him a number of import-export contracts for native rattan furniture, metalwork, and grass-cloth rugs. Wright himself was later to take full advantage of the contracts he made in Japan when, during the early 1960s, he designed a line of ceramics and glassware for production by the Yamato Porcelain Company. This line is remarkable for its blend of characteristic Wrightian shapes and strong Oriental influences.[54] The most enduring effects of the Asian trip were visible in Wright's personal aesthetic. He was particularly intrigued with Japan, for his visit there confirmed certain long-held artistic ideas and expanded his perceptions to envision new possibilities.

He was moved by the theatrical quality of the Japanese tea ceremony, by the seamless unity achieved in the traditional Japanese home between the house itself and its natural setting, and by the Japanese ability to blend natural tones and materials with striking colors in their designs. He found support for his own cherished ideas about the presentation of food in the care with which the Japanese made each dish into still-life. The effects of this first trip to Japan, and of a return visit in 1960, can be seen in all of Wright's late work, but they are perhaps nowhere more dramatically visible than in the design and construction of his estate in Garrison.

The Wrights had acquired the eighty-acre Garrison estate in 1941 as a weekend retreat, but now, during the postwar years, Wright spent an increasingly large proportion of his time there. In designing Dragon Rock, he was creating both a house and a way of life. The Garrison property slowly evolved from a simple rustic place to "get away from it all" into an embodiment of Wright's fully mature ideas about designs for living.

OPPOSITE
44. Dragon Rock, completed 1961
Wright flooded an abandoned stone quarry on his upstate New York property, laid out walking trails around it, and built his house into the rock above it.

Wright described Dragon Rock as a "prototype," a "designer's experiment." He wanted "to prove that a house of good contemporary design could be as livable as traditional ones; that it could be romantic, sentimental, even lovable…"[55] Starting with the landscape setting, Wright worked to "dramatize" nature. He was no enthusiast of nature unadorned, and spoke of the "typical monotony" it produces "unless man or the elements disturb the overall repetitive pattern."[56] Describing his efforts to "improve" upon nature—in terms that are strikingly similar to those used by eighteenth-century theorists of the Picturesque—Wright strove for an appearance of naturalness, achieved through considerable effort. He explored his property carefully to discover the best features of the landscape and then worked to highlight them through selective clearing and planting. He followed the natural contours of the land in laying out paths and vistas; he avoided straight lines and sought variety. Where certain trees, shrubs, or flowers appeared naturally, Wright cleared away other species to allow the chosen plants to propagate. On the other hand, when confronted with a large grove of hemlocks, he broke up the monotonous effect by introducing a group of birch trees for contrast.

Wright's property contained an abandoned stone quarry, into which he diverted a stream. The artificial pond this created was Dragon Rock's centerpiece. Around it he laid out two miles of walking trails, which were specifically planned for use at different times of day and during different seasons. Some were for single, others for double-file use. There was an autumn trail (richly colored foliage), a winter trail (mostly evergreens) and even a morning trail (featuring eastern light). The trails were of different lengths, and included places to pause and rest or reflect. There is a masterful variety of contrasting effects to be enjoyed along the trails: woods with meadows, fern groves with ponds, trees with boulders, and enclosed areas with long vistas.

In the midst of this controlled and dramatic environment, Wright built his house. Construction stretched over four years and was finally complete in 1961. Even to a generation familiar with Frank Lloyd Wright's "Falling Water," Dragon Rock is a remarkably ambitious and original house, literally cut into the side of the quarry and built on no less than eleven separate levels.[57] Living and dining areas were planned in one wing, and rooms for Wright's daughter, Ann, and a housekeeper were set in another. Wright himself slept in a separate but connected studio building with its own bath, fold-away kitchen, and terraces.

Thus, the house was divided into private and "public" areas. In the latter, the spaces are open and flowing. Visitors enter onto a small landing, pass down a flight of oak steps, and are immediately confronted with the two-story living/dining room and a panoramic view to the quarry and the falls outside. This central living area has a natural slate floor, a huge corner fireplace made of boulders, built-in seating, and a long, curving stone staircase which leads down to the dining area and kitchen on a lower level. A low counter divides the kitchen from the dining room.

OPPOSITE
45. Wright at Dragon Rock, 1962
Drawing on his experiences in the Far East, Wright designed Dragon Rock using aesthetic principles of continuity and contrast.

46. Dragon Rock and surroundings, 1962
Each level of Wright's house opens onto an outdoor terrace and partakes of carefully calculated views. These two-story windows, forming one side of the living/dining room, command a dramatic view of the quarry and waterfall.

Like the public rooms, the private areas incorporate natural features. There is a bath with a sheltered view of the quarry, and a tub complete with rocks and a miniature waterfall, as well as a private terrace with outdoor fireplace. Every level of the house, in fact, opens onto an outdoor terrace and partakes of carefully calculated views.

Drawing on his Far Eastern experiences, Wright relied on the aesthetic principles of continuity and contrast throughout. The rectilinear shapes of cut lumber contrasted with natural rock both inside the house and out; man-made fibers set off natural ones. The living room's slate floor continued through sliding glass doors to become the terrace, and a large uncut cedar tree supported the two-story dining room ceiling. Interestingly, Wright experimented, sometimes unsuccessfully, in combining raw natural and new synthetic materials throughout the house: styrofoam insulation is left exposed between the wood beams of the "den" ceiling, kitchen and bathroom partitions are constructed of plastic panels into which wild flowers from the property were embedded. Hemlock needles were pressed into wet epoxy wall paint to texture the living room and studio walls.

Wright sought throughout his career to create designs rich in tactile qualities. At Dragon Rock he created a multilayered sensual environment which revealed itself only over time. It was the bold site and dramatic vistas that most engaged the first-time visitor; only slowly did the more subtle details become apparent. Inside, Wright's attention to seemingly insignificant details is impressive. Lighting was controlled with theatrical precision from groups of centrally placed switches and dimmers. No two door handles are alike. In Japanese fashion, most decorative objects were normally kept out of sight, to be displayed only periodically in carefully arranged still-life groupings. Not surprisingly, Wright became very interested in the art of flower arranging, and provided a room for just that purpose.

Dragon Rock was designed as a theatrical spectacular that underwent seasonal transformations—much as scenery is changed between the acts of a play. During the warm months, drapes, upholstery, rugs, and accessories were coordinated to blend with outdoor tones in cool shades of green, blue, and white. For winter these were replaced by a complete second set of furnishings in warm reds and browns to contrast with the snow outside. Wright even extended this practice to the dining room chandelier, and tried to simplify these seasonal metamorphoses by making slipcovers reversible and by hanging cabinet doors on double hinges. One side of each door was painted white and the other red, so that each spring and fall they could easily be turned around.

Wright's love of novelty and his penchant for labor-saving devices found expression throughout the house. In the kitchen a counterbalanced shelf for the storage of glassware vanished into the ceiling over the buffet counter. Silver drawers in this same counter opened into both the kitchen and dining areas, and a dumbwaiter connected the front hall with a special shelf near the refrigerator.

Wright set about systematizing everything, sometimes to an extent that seems bizarre indeed. Each item in the kitchen had a specific and carefully labeled place. One very characteristic touch was Wright's menu planner. He prepared a large notebook of one hundred menus for his family. Each page contained a list of required supplies, preparation instructions, and the specific flatware, linen, glass, and ceramics needed for serving the meal. He specified not only the types of serving pieces that were needed, but their precise designs and colors as well. At the start of each week he would select all meals for the next seven days and arrange the appropriate pages in a separate notebook.

D ragon Rock grew from a design experiment to an obsession. Refrigerator shelves were labeled and ingredients arranged in the order in which they were to be used. Ann Wright recalls that her father insisted that the instructions in the book be followed exactly. Woe betide anyone who attempted to substitute blue for pink dishes! Wright also systemized entertaining. Guests always served themselves from the kitchen buffet from set seasonal menus: Chrysanthemum Duck was the autumn standard, curry for winter, and so on.

As happened so often in Wright's life, his penchant for machine-like domestic efficiency seemed, paradoxically, to make life more complex and inflexible. Instead of the "informality" he so professed, Wright had succeeded in creating a new sort of formality that expressed his own personality but infuriated those around him. Dragon Rock proved a difficult house in which to live. People tripped on the uneven stone floor, and fell down the rough stairs. The quarry site was damp, and wood began to deteriorate rapidly. The kitchen dumbwaiter and glassware shelf were cumbersome and broke often, and the "easy care" plastic partitions cracked and discolored. Ann Wright recalls hours spent vacuuming the rocks in the living room.

The estate became, in the words of Wright's biographer Marley Beers, the designer's lover and his friend. Dragon Rock was also a battleground, the site of an ongoing struggle between Wright's abstract concepts of modernity and efficiency and his uncompromising aesthetic standards. All of his experience is made visible in it: his early training in the theater; his life as a designer of furniture, ceramics, and accessories; the influence of his trips to the East and his rediscovery of nature. As is so often the case with such "demonstration" houses as LeCorbusier's Villa Savoie or Frank Lloyd Wright's Falling Water, Dragon Rock is flawed as a practical dwelling. But Russel Wright's house, despite its excesses and extremes, is far less an object than each of them; Dragon Rock has a gentler personality, and seems far more at peace with its surroundings than do either the Corbusier or Frank Lloyd Wright houses.

OPPOSITE
47. Wright at Dragon Rock, 1962
Wright wields a broom; below are the kitchen and dining room, divided by a low counter. Silverware drawers in the counter opened into both kitchen and dining areas, and above it, a counterbalanced shelf for glassware could be lowered for use or raised to disappear into the ceiling. Throughout Dragon Rock, Wright's love of novelty and labor-saving devices is evident.

Earlier Domestic Interiors

Wright's work at Garrison clearly demonstrates the point to which his ideas had evolved by the mid 1960s. Looking back at the series of apartments and houses he built for himself and his family in earlier years provides an instructive contrast that indicates just how far he had come. Wright designed his first apartment, over the shop at 135 East 35th Street, in 1931. Working with two rooms in what once had been a hayloft, he created an environment for himself and Mary so unusual that it resists general description. Wright himself referred to the apartment as "modernized Victorian," but most of its elements seem to have been derived either from the theater or from the Hollywood sound stage.[58] The bedroom was painted dark red with white trim; floor-to-ceiling classical columns opened to provide closet space. Torch lamps, masks, and lyre-back chairs in white completed the ensemble. The living room was more restrained, with dark brown walls, white trim, and Biedermeier-inspired furniture upholstered in both solid and plaid fabric. The total effect was not unlike a set for a Cocteau play. Yet it reflects both the free-wheeling humor and the fantasy of Wright's early work, as well as indicating the degree to which the theater had permeated his sensibility.

The penthouse apartment in the Concord Hotel at 130 East 40th Street, into which the Wrights moved around 1933, could not have been more different in character. Now it was the influence of the Bauhaus and of Wright's industrial designer colleagues that dominated, and the apartment became an advertisement for Wright and his work.[59] The bright colors had vanished and all was smooth, sleek, and functional. Rubber tile was used on the floors, and the walls were painted a neutral gray. The furniture was constructed of metal tubing and industrial materials, and the built-in cabinets contained not only domestic items, but equipment for the display and sale of Wright's designs. The only recognizably Wrightian features in this machine-age interior were the increasing number of gadgets and the pony skin chair that was later shown at the Museum of Modern Art.

Wright's next apartment, at 7 Park Avenue, was much warmer and more traditionally luxurious.[60] Wood paneling was used extensively, along with Wright furniture designs. Only in the bedroom did echoes of the 35th Street apartment survive—in the hot pink walls, green carpet, and magenta drapes and upholstery.

More historically significant was the house at 221 East 48th Street, which the Wrights remodeled around 1949.[61] Wright converted a standard New York brownstone into a combination home, office, and rental property. The lower floor was devoted to business, with a reception area, a conference room, and a large work space that occupied an S-shaped extension added to the rear of the main house. Six-foot windows allowed this indoor workroom to be filled with the light

OPPOSITE
48. The Wrights' first apartment, 1931
Russel and Mary Wright's first apartment was located over their workshop on 35th Street in New York. The designer dubbed its highly theatrical style "Modernized Victorian." This photograph appeared in House Beautiful in 1934.

NEXT PAGE
49. Second apartment, ca. 1934
For his second New York apartment, Wright abandoned the stylish excess of his first home in favor of a restrained modernity. The decor here reflects Wright's new consciousness of himself as an industrial designer.

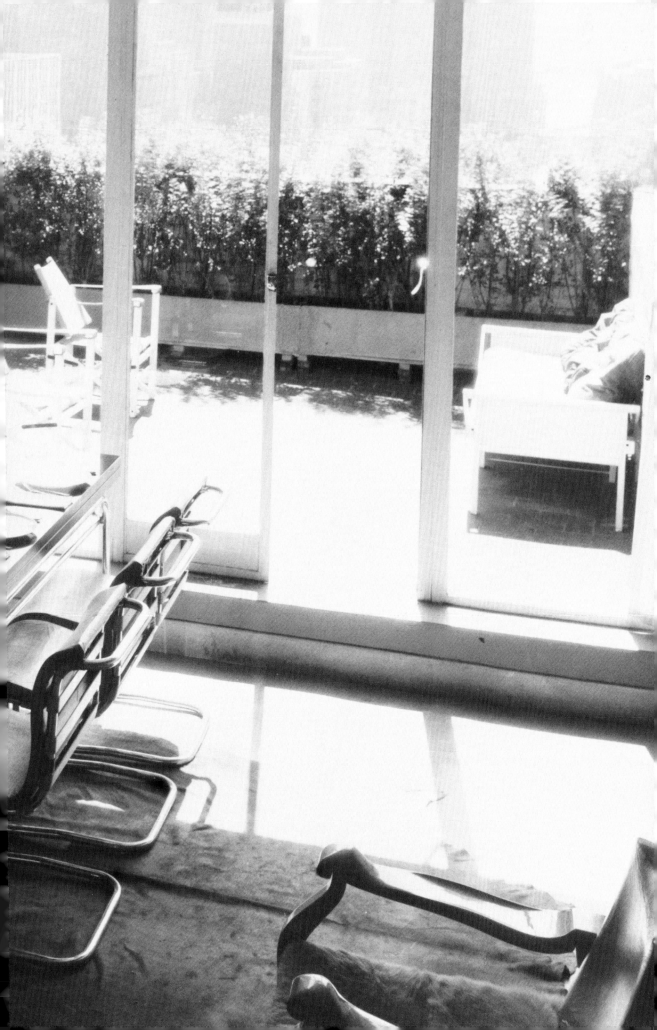

and color of the garden outside. Executed a full eight years before Wright's eastern trip, the reception and conference areas were cool and serene, almost Oriental in feeling. Wood paneling contrasted with plastic partitions. Lighting was carefully controlled, and flowers, arranged in Bauer pottery vases, were strategically placed. To a considerable extent, the lower floor of the 48th Street house was a trial run for Dragon Rock.

Upstairs, the living quarters broke less decisively with the past. Furniture from the Wrights' previous apartments was mixed with new designs, space-saving closets, and built-in cabinets. The spaces were imaginatively treated, but somewhat cluttered. The contrast between the office and the living floors is easily explained. Because Russel and Mary Wright worked so closely together, some scholars have suggested that their designs were in most cases collaborative, their styles interchangeable. But a study of the Wrights' apartments and a comparison of them to Russel's work at Garrison after Mary's death reveals a number of differences in their aesthetic personalities. Mary, whose work may be seen upstairs in the 48th Street house, and in family areas of the earlier apartments, seems to have been far less adventurous than her husband. She was not so much a designer as a homemaker, favoring traditional furniture and accessories, floral patterns, and a comfortable fussiness in decor. Russel was more inclined to experiment, to blend natural and artificial materials, to try striking color combinations and theatrical ensembles. He grew as a designer by living constantly with and in his work.

By the 1960s, Wright was a year-round resident of Garrison, and closely involved with the local community. He joined the Garrison Landing Association, a group of residents devoted to upgrading the condition of the deteriorated Hudson River shoreline, and became deeply involved with fund-raising and public relations. For three years, beginning in 1963, he planned an annual Garrison Landing Festival to draw public attention to the history and ecology of the river and to the dangers of the current shoreline condition.

Word of the Garrison project spread, and Wright was soon working as a consultant for New York State at Bear Mountain State Park. In 1967, Under Secretary of the Interior Stanley Cain had dinner at Dragon Rock, and shortly thereafter he arranged for Wright to visit Washington to study the park system there. Cain had originally hoped that Wright would agree to design a new park for the District of Columbia, but Wright proposed instead an imaginative scheme for the reuse of existing parks. Congressional funding was secured, and the innovative "Summer in the Parks" program was launched in 1968. Wright's program of trips, crafts, concerts, and sports, all organized at the neighborhood level, was tremendously popular; it continues in only slightly altered form to this day.

50. East 48th Street townhouse, ca. 1949

The upper floors of the Wrights' brownstone townhouse were re-modelled as living quarters while the ground level housed Wright's office and design studio. The camera is looking toward the dining area and the glassed in kitchen. At left is the storage wall for music with doors closed. Furniture is on casters for easy mobility.

NEXT PAGE

51. East 48th Street townhouse addition, ca. 1949

Wright's S-shaped addition included a reception area, conference room, and a large, light-filled studio.

His work for the Parks Service was to have a crucial effect on the fate of Dragon Rock. From the start, he had envisioned the estate as both a residence and a demonstration of his ideas and had been concerned that it one day be opened for public enjoyment. His parks experience gave him the idea of making it into a public center for nature and design studies. By the early 1970s, plans were well advanced, and, after considering a number of alternatives, Wright deeded his acreage, with the exception of the house itself, to the Nature Conservancy, a non-profit conservation organization.

The new center was dubbed Manitoga, and plans were drawn for a large nature study building. Wright and his assistants marked trails, planned programs, and trained guides, stressing the theme of a direct, sensory experience of nature. Visitors were to be accompanied along the trails in small groups and encouraged to hug trees, to lie on the ground, to wade in streams, to sing and to meditate. Programs included music in the woods, and an Indian "Festival of Light" with dancing and storytelling. Unfortunately, Wright did not live to see his ideas in action. He died of cancer in December 1976, just as the programs were becoming established. The Nature Conservancy has continued to care for Manitoga and operate it according to Wright's plans.

During the course of his extraordinarily wide-ranging career, Wright worked with comparatively few themes. His major concern was to discover and define harmonies between man and nature, between the natural and the man-made worlds. As a designer he was engaged in combining organic and mechanical forms, in blending traditional with machine-made materials, neutral tints with striking colors, practical utility with witty expression. Behind these balanced contrasts lay Wright's struggle to resolve the conflicting demands of standardized efficiency and artistic expression, rational systematization and romantic individuality, American tradition and international innovation, financial gain and artistic integrity.

Wright ranks with this nation's most original, inventive, and influential designers, a complex man whose great seriousness of purpose contributed to his considerable successes and failures alike. His life and work opened the eyes of millions of ordinary Americans to the aesthetic possibilities of everyday life. So many of his ideas have been assumed as natural cultural developments, or have been appropriated as the provinces of specific industries as movements, that his own name has been largely forgotten today. But we need only look around us at the way we live our daily lives to perceive Wright's influence, and to appreciate the breadth of his innovative, original talent.

Notes

[1] Wright's mother was Harryet Morris Crigler, a descendant of Robert Morris and William Whipple. His father was Willard Wright, son of a celebrated Quaker abolitionist. Russel had one sister.

[2] Russel Wright, manuscript autobiography (preserved at Manitoga), 5.

[3] By 1923 Woodstock had become a thriving art colony. While the Byrdcliffe Colony for the Arts and Crafts was no longer active, its memory was still fresh in local minds. Since 1906, Woodstock had been the home of the Art Students' League Summer School. By the mid-teens, Hervey White's farm had emerged as an artists' residence and a center of literary and political discussion. White had organized the first Maverick Festival in 1917, and it was so popular that it was repeated each year until 1931. At first it was little more than a community costume party, but by the mid-1920s the Festival had evolved into something more serious. It offered regularly scheduled chamber concerts by New York musicians, presented Shakespeare plays, and, in 1920, presented the premiere of Edna St. Vincent Millay's antiwar play, *Aria da Capo*.

[4] Max Reinhardt's production of Karl Vollmoeller's pantomime *The Miracle* opened in New York in November of 1924. Bel Geddes had entirely transformed the interior of the Century Theatre to resemble a medieval cathedral, with acoustic and visual effects that were among the most ambitious ever attempted. The result was a widely acclaimed spectacle.

[5] Mary Wright had brought to their marriage a "dowry" of much-needed capital and important connections.

[6] Additional caricatures included Paul Whiteman in wood, Mary Pickford in rhinestones and papier-mâché, George Bernard Shaw in aluminum sheeting and bottle brushes, and the Prince of Wales in pink soap. The Herbert Hoover mask was published in the *New Review*, 1 (1930). None of the original masks are known to survive.

[7] Wright quoted in "Adventure in Aluminum," *Industrial Design*, 7 (May 1960), 54.

[8] The nature of Wright's public in the early 1930s may be gleaned from a passage in Mary McCarthy's *The Group* (New York, 1954) in which it is reported that the favorite wedding present received by one of the novel's most sophisticated characters not long after graduation from Vassar in 1933 was a Russel Wright cocktail shaker of aluminum and oak.

[9] See, for example, Ruth Averell Meigs, "Accents on Accessories," *Creative Art*, 9 (December 1931), 475-6; *American Home*, 10 (July 1933), 57; 11 (January 1934), 60-2. Martin Greif illustrates a number of these pieces in *Depression Modern, the Thirties Style in America* (New York, 1975), 168-9.

[10] Wright, "Adventure in Aluminum," 54.

[11] *Twelfth Exhibition of Contemporary American Industrial Art*, New York, Metropolitan Museum of Art, 13 October-22 November 1931. For additional information see Richard R. Bach, "Contemporary American Industrial Art: Twelfth Exhibition," *Metropolitan Museum Bulletin*, 26 (October 1931), 226-9. For the exhibition in Philadelphia see Joseph Downs, "Design for the Machine," *Pennsylvania Museum Bulletin*, 27 (March 1932), 115-9.

[12] These concepts, developed early in the century by Earnest Calkins and Ralph Holden, were first applied in the automobile industry by such businessmen as Alfred P. Sloan of General Motors. Calkins' ideas were later refined and expanded by Egmont Arens and Roy Sheldon in their book *Consumer Engineering: A Technique for Prosperity* (New York, 1932).

[13] Teague's 1939 piano is illustrated in Greif, *Depression Modern*, 160. Around 1930 Norman Bel Geddes also designed a modern piano in wood (see Bel Geddes's autobiography, *Horizons* [Boston, 1932], 135.) Its style is not dissimilar to that of Wright's instrument.

[14] See the *Architectural Record*, 74 (December 1933), 479-82.

[15] *Art in Our Time*, Tenth Anniversary Exhibition, Museum of Modern Art, New York. Wright was the only American invited to display furniture in the exhibition. His chair, made of wood and organically shaped, contrasted dramatically with the chairs by Le Corbusier, Mies, and Breuer, with which it was shown.

[16] Catalogues of the Conant Ball line are preserved in the Wright archives at Syracuse University. See also *House and Garden*, 68 (September 1935), 58-9 for a printed advertisement of the line.

[17] *Ibid.*

[18] Bel Geddes had pioneered the use of a designer's name as a sales tool in 1930 with his Philco radio and applied the concept again, most effectively, in 1933 in connection with a new design for a gas stove. In 1935 Loewy also used the technique in marketing his Sears Coldspot refrigerator. For details about Wright's exploitation of his name see: "Russel Wright Does Not Advertise, But Many Ads Give Him Top Billing," *Advertising Age*, 19 November 1951.

[19] *American Modern* was also originally produced in a warm white. During the war, Bean Brown was replaced by Black Chutney, and Cedar Green was added to the line. Cantaloupe and Glacier Blue were added in the 1950s.

[20] In his autobiography Wright mentions the influence of surrealism on his exhibition designs for the 1939 World's Fair (p. 35). Surrealist elements also appear in his 1939 displays for the American Handkerchief Company.

[21] Manny Farber, "Like a Rock Cast in the Sea," *New Republic*, 111 (20 November 1944), 661-2.

[22] *Time*, 52 (19 August 1948).

[23] "On and Off the Avenue," *New Yorker*, 25 (17 September 1949), 82.

[24] See "Mob Scene Over Modern," *Retailing Home Furnishings*, 24 June 1947, 45.

[25] Wright's exacting exploration of the company's merchandising process is described in "Designers of Showroom and Displays Study Sales Methods," *Architectural Record*, 86 (July 1933), 38; and "Silent Salesmanship," *Art and Design*, 26 (January 1939), 23-6.

[26] Autobiography, 35.

[27] The dissolution of the Wright/Richards partnership is documented in the Wright archives at Syracuse. The original firm, Russel Wright Associates, was reorganized in 1937 into Russel Wright and Associates (a creative group headed by Russel) and Wright Accessories. Mary Wright, Richards, Eugene Morganthau, and Hans Forscheimer were the stockholders of the latter corporation; Russel was listed only as an employee. This arrangement was planned to separate design from manufacturing and distribution, allowing Wright time to concentrate on independent consulting work. In 1939 an even more decisive split seemed desirable, and Richards bought out Mary Wright's interest in Wright Accessories. In so doing he became the sole manufacturing and sales agent for Wright's lamps, ceramics, and aluminum pieces.

[28] See Russel Wright, "Art Education in the American Way," *Design*, 42 (March 1941), 5; and Wright, "Industry Looks at Art," in the same issue, 23.

[29] Speech to New York Fashion Group, reprinted in Greif, *Depression Modern*, 43.

[30] This and the following quotations are from a draft of the *American Way* sales manual, preserved in the Wright papers at Syracuse.

[31] Mrs. Roosevelt delivered a short speech at Macy's on 21 September 1940.

[32] "Machine Made Pottery Has a New Look," *New York Times*, 15 August 1946.

[33] See *House Beautiful*, 82 (October 1940), 68-9; *Magazine of Art*, 33 (November 1940), 626-9; *House and Garden*, 78 (November 1940), supp. 34-5.

[34] Two thirds of the capital for *American Way* was Wright's. The architect Michael Hare and others put up the remainder. Wright insisted in paying back his investors in full, a task which took ten years.

[35] The *Guide to Easier Living* was published by Simon and Schuster. The text had been ghostwritten by Ruth Goode, and was based on research and ideas developed by Russel and Mary Wright.

[36] *New Yorker*, 27 (12 May 1951), 129-30.

[37] Until 1946 Wright was under exclusive contract to design dinnerware only for Raymor. The expiration of this agreement was a further stimulus to the creation of new designs.

[38] *Casual China* was produced in Ice Blue, Forest Green, Avocado, and Lemon Yellow. Lettuce Green, Charcoal, Ripe Apricot, Pink Sherbet, Parsley Green, Cantaloupe, Oyster Grey, Aqua, Brick Red, and Grey/Blue were added in 1951. In 1959 several floral patterns were offered.

[39] See "New China is Hard to Break," *New York Times*, 10 December 1947.

[40] *Highlight* was produced in Snow Glaze, Citron, Blueberry, Nutmeg, Pepper, and White.

[41] Wright's only competitor in the design of high-quality plastic dinnerware was Irving Harper, working for George Nelson. For a discussion of early Melmac see: "Plastics on the Table," *Industrial Design*, 1 (April 1954), 63-70.

[42] Wright hated to travel and does not seem to have visited Europe in the early 1950s. It is possible, nevertheless, that he knew and absorbed the lessons of the contemporary furniture being produced there. It may be significant that Wright, in an exception to his usual practice, decorated certain areas of his house on 48th Street with Aalto furniture.

[43] See Frances Heard, "Modern Gets More Human All the Time," *House Beautiful*, 93 (June 1951), 98-9; Mary Davis Gillies, "You'll Enjoy This New Furniture," *Mc-Calls*, 78 (May 1951), 48-52.

[44] The speech was delivered in July 1976. I am grateful to Ray Spillman for allowing me to consult his tape recording of it.

[45] The *Good Design* exhibitions were held alternately in New York and Chicago at six-month intervals between 1950 and 1955. *American Modern* dinnerware and Wright's 1950 Samsonite folding chair were included in the first exhibition, and new designs were represented each year thereafter. Wright's *Residential* plastic was selected in 1954 for inclusion in the Museum of Modern Art's *100 Museum Selections from "Good Design."*

[46] Wright had also been included, of course, in a number of exhibitions at the start of his career, among them *Design for the Machine* at the Philadelphia Art Museum in 1932, *Contemporary American Industrial Art* at the Metropolitan shortly before, and the Museum of Modern Art's 10th Anniversary exhibition in 1939. But this constituted nowhere near the institutional attention he was to receive in the mid-1950s.

[47] As an activist president, he worked to expand the Society's activities and to open membership in the formerly exclusive group to younger designers.

[48] "The 100 'Best-Dressed' Products," *Fortune*, 59 (April 1959), 135-41. The poll was conducted by the Institute of Design at the Illinois Institute of Technology.

[49] See Wright's article, "The Case for Color in School Furniture," *Interiors*, 115 (April 1955), 160ff; and "Russel Wright Classroom Furniture," *Architectural Forum*, 102 (January 1955), 224.

[50] Both the Sterling and Iroquois firms applied custom decoration to Wright ceramics for their commercial clients. These decorative elements were not, however, of Wright's design.

[51] The Harker line featured engraved white flowers (clover) on backgrounds of Meadow Green, Coral Sand, Golden Spice, and Charcoal. (This firm also produced the faceplate for Wright's General Electric clock.) The Knowles *Esquire* pieces, sold until 1962, were an even more dramatic departure. Floral patterns—Botanica, Queen Anne's Lace, Solar, Seeds, and Grass—were stamped in pale tones on a light-colored matte body. The *Esquire* line shows a definite Oriental influence, both in the shape of many of the pieces as well as in some of the decorative patterns.

[52] For use at Garrison, Wright designed and had custom-made a set of transparent Melamine dinnerware in which actual leaves from the woods surrounding the house were cast in the plastic.

[53] Wright devotes over one hundred pages to the trip in his autobiography. I have not been able to locate a copy of the official report.

[54] A prototype was also produced using Wrightian shapes with a richly textured orange and black glaze of traditional Japanese inspiration.

[55] Diane Cochrane, "Designer for All Seasons," *Industrial Design*, 23 (March/April 1976), 49.

[56] Wright, *Woodland Paths*, manuscript dated 5 November 1969 and preserved at Manitoga, 1.

[57] The similarity between Dragon Rock and such houses by Frank Lloyd Wright (no relation) as Falling Water is no coincidence. By the early 1950s both the designer and the architect were accustomed to being confused in the public mind. Shortly after Mary's death, Russel asked his business manager, Herbert Honig, to set up a meeting with the architect, whose work he had come to admire. In 1952 Russel traveled to Taliesin and spent a long weekend with the architect. In spite of professed mutual admiration, no sustained correspondence or relationship developed from this meeting.

[58] See "A Designer at Home," *House Beautiful*, 75 (June 1934), 31-4.

[59] See *London Studio*, 117 (June 1939), 30; Greif, *Depression Modern*, 64.

[60] See "Living in a Laboratory," *Interiors*, 102 (June 1943), 32-5.

[61] See "Idyll on 48th Street," *Interiors*, 109 (September 1949), 88-95.

List of Selected Designs

Home Furniture

Heywood-Wakefield Company, Gardner, Massachusetts
1933-34   Line of upholstered furniture

Conant Ball Company, Gardner, Massachusetts
1935   *Modern Living* line (later called *American Modern* line)
1936   *Blonde Modern* line

American Hickory Company, Indiana
1940 (-1942?)   *Old Hickory* line

Monitor and Sprague & Carleton Companies
1940   *American Way* furniture

Sears Roebuck, Chicago, Illinois
1942   *Knockdown* line of furniture

Statton Furniture Company, Hagerstown, Maryland
1950   *Easier Living* line (1949-52, exclusive RW client for wooden furniture; line sold through Modernage, New York)

Commercial Furniture

Colgate Aircraft Corporation, Amityville, New York
1945   Folding metal furniture

Shwayder Corporation, Denver and Detroit
1950   *Samsonite* Folding metal chairs and tables
1955   School furniture

Featherweight Aluminum Products, Montreal
1955   Folding metal furniture

Lamps

Wright Accessories/Raymor, New York City
1939-47   Miscellaneous lamps

Mutual Sunset Lamp Company, New York City
1946-49   Miscellaneous lamps

Acme Fluorescent, New York City
1946-49   Miscellaneous lamps

Amplex Corporation
1949   Swivel lamp

Fairmount Lamps, Philadelphia
1951   Table and floor lamps

Ceramic Dinnerware

Steubenville Pottery, East Liverpool, Ohio
1937   *American Modern* (Introduced 1939, marketed until ca. 1959, distributed by Raymor)

Iroquois China Company, Syracuse, New York
1946   *Casual China* (Redesigned 1950 and 1959 with addition of floral decoration, distributed by Garrison Products, New York, 1946-48)

Sterling China Company
1948   Vitreous hotel china

Paden City Pottery, Paden City, West Virginia
1951   *Highlight* combined ceramic and glass line (Distributed by Justin Tharaud, New York, 1951-53)

Harker Pottery Company, East Liverpool, Ohio
1951   *White Clover*

Edwin M. Knowles Pottery Company, East Liverpool, Ohio
1956   *Esquire Collection* (Sold until 1962, mostly through chain and discount stores)

Schmidt International (Yamato Porcelain Co., Tajmi, Japan)
1963   Line of porcelain dinnerware

Plastic Dinnerware

American Cyanamid, New York
1945   Prototype set of Melamine dinnerware

General American Transportation
1949   *Meladur* (Commercial production of American Cyanamid designs)

Northern Industrial Chemical, Boston
1953   *Residential*
1959   *Flair*

Ideal Toy Company
1955   *Idealware* polyethylene (Marketed until 1962, line included set of children's dishes)

Paper Dinnerware

Sutherland Paper
    1959   Paper plates, etc.
Bowes Industries, Chicago
    1950   Line of paper plates and cups

Flatware

Wright Accessories
    1933   Experimental set of silver flatware
Englishtown Cutlery, New York and New Jersey
    1946   Line of stainless flatware with plastic
                    handles
John Hull Cutlery
    1951   *American Modern*
    1953   *Highlight*
    1950-58   Miscellaneous cutlery designs, all made
                    in Japan

Holloware and Miscellaneous Serving Accessories

Wright Accessories/Raymor
    1929-35   Miscellaneous designs in pewter,
                    chrome, and aluminum
Klise Woodenware, Grand Rapids, Michigan
    1935   *Oceana* line of free-form wooden
                    serving pieces (distributed by Wright
                    Accessories/Raymor)
Chase Brass, New York
    1930s-1944 Corn set, ice buckets, beer pitcher
Century Metalcraft, New York
    1940-44   Aluminum bowls, trays, ice buckets,
                    etc.
Aluminum Goods Manufacturing Corporation, Manitowoc, Wisconsin
    1946-48   *Stove-to-Table* line (Mirro)
Ravensware, Brooklyn
    1955   Aluminum and pewter pieces:
                    ice buckets, trays, chafing dishes,
                    thermos bottles
Bauer Pottery, Atlanta, Georgia
    1943-46   Line of freeform "art" ceramics
                    (sold through Wright Accessories/
                    Raymor)
Duraware Corporation, New York
    1964-65   Plastic trays, buckets, colanders, etc.

Glass

Century Metalcraft
    1945   Set of glassware
                    (contract sold to American Crystal,
                    1947)
Appleman Art Glass, North Hackensack, New Jersey
    1946-52   Bent glass serving pieces
Fostoria Glass, Moundsville, West Virginia
    1946-48   Miscellaneous glass pieces
American Crystal, Washington, Pennsylvania
    1947   Line of uncolored glassware
Imperial Glass
    1949   *Flair* line: 3 groups of tumblers in
                    clear, colored, and seed glass
    ?   *Pinch* line to accompany *Casual China*
                    in pink, green, smoke, ruby
Morgantown Glass Guild
    1951   *American Modern* colored and shaped
                    glasses
Bartlett Collins Glass Company, Sapulpa, Oklahoma
    1957-58   Stencil designs
(see also Paden City pottery line)

Appliances

Silex Corporation
    1942   Alcohol stove and coffee maker
Amtra Trading Corporation, New York
    1946   Electric iron—produced ?
Ladge Electric, Boston, Mass.
    1947   Commercial popcorn warmer
General Electric
    1953   Ceramic-faced clock
Cornwall Corporation, Boston, Mass.
    1958-61   Electro-thermal serving trays
Peerless Electric, New York
    1955   *Broil Quick*

Fabrics and Surfaces

Lecock and Company, New York
    1946-48   *American Modern* table linen
Cohen, Hall, Marx, and Co., New York
    1946-48   Plastic table mats and cloths
Hedwin Corporation, Baltimore, Maryland
    1946-54   Plastic table mats
Frank and Sadev, New York
    1948-50   Napkins and table mats
Simtex Mills, New York
    1950   Plaid table cloths

Art Loom Carpets, Philadephia
1934   Carpets for Heywood-Wakefield line
1951   Carpets
Everfast Fabrics, New York
1951   Drapery fabric
Comprehensive Fabrics, New York
1951   Plastic table mats
Lumite Division, Chicopee Manufacturing, New York
1951   Upholstery fabric for Statton line
Aristocrat Leather, New York
1951   Vinyl table mats
Patchogue Mills, New York
1951   Rugs and table linens
Foster Textile Mills, Chicago
1952-57   Fabrics
Edson, Inc., New York
1954-55   Fabrics
Dupont, Wilmington, Delaware
1954-57   *Fabrilite* vinyl upholstery colors
American Olean Tile, New York
1957   Tile

Packaging
Calvert Distilling (Seagram)
1955   Calvert Reserve decanter
Proctor and Gamble, Cincinnati, Ohio
1959   "Big Top Peanut Butter" jar and label
Hunt Foods, Fullerton, California
1959-61   Catsup bottle and label
Cresca, New York
1961   New bottle and label

Domestic Interiors
RW Beekman Place Apartment, New York City, 1929

RW East 35th Street Apartment/Showroom, New York City, 1933.

RW East 40th Street Penthouse/Studio, New York City, 1934

RW 7 Park Avenue Penthouse Apartment, New York City, 1938

RW East 48th Street House, 1949.

Donald Slesinger Residence, Croton-on-Hudson, New York, Wright and Snow architects

Manitoga (formerly Dragon Rock), house largely complete by 1956, property acquired 1941.

Commercial Interiors
Gimbel Brothers, New York
1932   Redesign of street floor
Wright Accessories, 35th Street, New York
1932   Showroom
Restaurant de Relle, 400 Madison Avenue, New York
1933   Cocktail lounge
George Bijur Office, New York
1935   Office interior
Wilkes-Barre Lace Company, New York
1936   Showroom
International Handkerchief Company, New York
1939   Showroom
New York World's Fair, New York
1939   Focal Food exhibit
            Mental Hygiene exhibit
            Guiness Stout exhibit
            Fashion Show
            New York Department Stores exhibit
Sak's 34th Street, New York
1944   Redesign of fourth floor
Statton Furniture Company, Grand Rapids, Michigan
1950   Showroom
Brass Rail Restaurants, New York
1962   Self-service restaurant—
            prototype design
Shun Lee Dynasty, New York
1966   Restaurant interior

Miscellaneous
Wurlitzer
1932   KRW piano, accordion, radios
Trimount Vending Machine, 1933
Mergenthaler Linotype Machine, early 1930s
Fashion Designs
Leather table accessories

Selected Chronological Bibliography

Naylor, Blanche. "American Design Process." *Design*, 33 (September 1931), 82-89.

Meigs, Ruth Averill. "Accents on Accessories." *Creative Art*, 9 (December 1931), 475-82.

"Serving Accessories." *American Home*, 10 (July 1933), 57.

McFadden, R.S. "Designers' Ability Salvages Waste." *Design*, 35 (September 1933), 20-22.

"Restaurant Du Relle." *Architectural Record*, 74 (December 1933), 479.

New York, Museum of Modern Art. *Machine Art*. (Exhibition, 1934).

Wright, Russel. "An Honest Expression of Present-Day Living." *American Home*, 11 (January 1934), 60-62.

"A Designer at Home." *House Beautiful*, 75 (April 1934), 30-33.

Wright, Russel. "A Guide to Buying Modern." *Arts and Decoration*, 42 (February 1935), 26-29.

"Designers Today: Russel Wright." *London Studio*, 109 (June 1935), 317-23.

"Modern American." *House and Garden*, 68 (September 1935), 58-59.

Sironen, Marta K. *A History of American Furniture*. Edited by N. I. Bienenstock. East Stroudsburg, Pa., 1936. 145-46.

Wright, Russel. "Combined Living-Recreation Room." *Architectural Forum*, 67 (October 1937), 283-85.

Wright, Russel. "Bedroom Comfort." *House and Garden*, 73 (April 1938), 108-110.

Wright, Russel, and Snow, Richard Boring. "A House on the Beach and a House by a Stream." *Country Life* [New York], 74 (May 1938), 84-87.

Wright, Russel. *Home Furnishings at the Fair*. New York: World's Fair Marketing Bulletin, 1939.

"Interior Combining Office and Living Room." *London Studio*, 117 (January 1939), 30.

"For Resting Your Skis." *Esquire* (January 1939), 38.

"Yacht Club." *Esquire* (August 1939), 88.

"Silent Salesmanship: Display Problems at International Handkerchief Company." *Art and Industry*, 26 (January 1939), 23-26.

"International Handkerchief Company Showroom." *Architectural Record*, 86 (July 1939), 38.

"Russel Wright." *Current Biography* (New York, 1940 and 1950).

"American Way." *House Beautiful*, 82 (October 1940), 68-69.

Watson, J. "American Way." *Magazine of Art*, 33 (November 1940), 626-29.

"All American Design." *House and Garden*, 78 (November 1940), supp. 34-35.

Wright, Russel. "Art Education the American Way." *Design*, 42 (March 1941), 5.

Wright, Russel. "Industry Looks at Art." *Design*, 42 (March 1941), 23.

Wright, Russel. "Bedroom." *Architectural Forum*, 77 (September 1942), 128-29.

Wright, Russel. "Living in a Laboratory." *Interiors*, 117 (June 1943), 32-35.

Wright, Russel. "How Will You Live Tomorrow?" *Better Homes and Gardens*, 23 (September 1944), 16-17.

Farber, Manny. "Like a Rock Cast in the Sea." *New Republic*, 111 (20 November 1944), 661-62.

"Russel and Mary Wright: Snapshot." *Interiors*, 118 (December 1944), 56-66.

Wright, Russel. "Bedrooms for Grown-Ups." *Better Homes and Gardens*, 23 (February 1945), 18-19.

"Russel Wright: Portrait." *Architectural Forum*, 82 (April 1945), 62.

"Meet Russel Wright." *House Beautiful*, 87 (May 1945), 79.

Kaufmann, Edgar, Jr. "Russel Wright: American Designer." *American Magazine of Art*, 41 (April 1948), 144-45.

"Conference and Display Room in New York." *Interiors* (August 1940), 101.

"Idyll on 48th Street." *Interiors*, 109 (September 1949), 88-95.

"Russel Wright." *Interiors*, 110 (November 1950), 99.

Wright, Russel, and Wright, Mary. *A Guide to Easier Living*. New York, 1951.

Gillies, Mary Davis. "You'll Love Living with This New Furniture." *McCalls*, 78 (May 1951), 48-52.

Heard, Frances. "Modern Gets More Human All the Time." *House Beautiful*, 93 (June 1951), 98-99.

Wright, Russel. "A Few Realistic Suggestions." *Interiors*, 111 (December 1951), 90-105.

Ritter, Chris. "An Interior View: Russel Wright." *Art Digest*, 27 (15 November 1952), 8-9.

"Wright's Highlights." *Interiors*, 112 (February 1953), 104.

Byerly, Florence. "Chart Your Way to 'Easier Living.'" *Better Homes and Gardens*, 31 (April 1953), 57-63.

"Russel Wright Portrait." *Interiors*, 114 (September 1954), 57.

Wright, Russel. "The Case for Color in School Furniture." *Interiors*, 115 (April 1955), 170 ff.

"Russel Wright Selects Industrial Fabric for Home Use." *American Fabrics*, 38 (1956), 38.

Wright, Russel. "Goldmine in Southeast Asia." *Interiors*, 116 (August 1956), 94-101.

Wright, Russel. "Any Man Can Keep House." *Woman's Home Companion*, 83 (September 1956), 50-51.

"Adventure in Aluminum." *Industrial Design*, 7 (May 1960), 54-56.

Gueft, Olga. "Dragon Rock." *Interiors*, 121 (September 1961), 100-111.

Grehan, Farrell. "A Wonderful House to Live In." *Life*, 52 (16 March 1962), 74-83.

Streichler, Jerry. *The Consultant Designer in American Industry*. New York University, Ph.D. dissertation, 1963.

"Shun Lee Dynasty, N.Y." *Interior Design*, 37 (April 1966), 194-97.

Greif, Martin. *Depression Modern: The 30s Style in America*. New York, 1975.

Bush, Donald. *The Streamlined Decade*. New York, 1975.

Cochrane, Diane. "Designer for All Seasons." *Industrial Design*, 23 (March/April 1976), 46-51.

Gueft, Olga. "Remembering Russel Wright." *Interiors*, 136 (May 1977), 74.

Greif, Martin. "Tribute to Russel Wright." *Craft Horizons*, 77 (August 1977), 44.

Meikle, Jeffrey L. *Twentieth Century Limited: Industrial Design in America, 1925-39*. Philadelphia, 1979.

Archival Sources:

Russel Wright papers (79 boxes), Arents Research Library, Syracuse University.

Miscellaneous files and papers are preserved in the offices of the Nature Conservancy at Manitoga and in the personal files of Ms. Marley Beers.

Photographic Credits

Berenice Abbott: 4.

Robert Disraeli: 2.

Courtney Frisse: Cover, 6, 10, 20, 32, 33, 35, 38, 40, 42.

Farrell Grehan: 27, 45-47.

Paulus Leeser: 15, 19, 30, 31, 36.

Steven Tucker: 18, 29, 34, 37.

Collection Credits

American Decorative Arts—Chris Kennedy: 38.

George Arents Research Library for Special Collections at Syracuse University (photographs): 4, 5, 7-9, 12-14, 16, 17, 21-26, 28, 39, 43, 49, 51.

Marley Beers (photographs): 1, 3, 11, 27, 41, 45-47, 50.

Depression Modern, N.Y., N.Y.: 6.

The Nature Conservancy: 44.

Paul F. Walter: Cover, 2, 10, 15, 19, 20, 30-33, 35, 36, 40 (chair), 42.

Ann Wright: 18, 29, 34, 37, 40 (table).

All numbers listed above refer to illustration numbers.